AF316696

Praise for Safar

This book tells an unforgettable story of how hardship and adversity can temper a human being like true steel and provide wisdom and insight on the other side. Read it for the story, but stay for the advice on how to live a more beautiful and productive life.

Nick Morgan, PhD, Communication and Speech Coach,
Former Fellow at Harvard's Kennedy School of Government,
and author

What a lovely memoir and life story from Ravi. This book is filled with relatable stories that can only come from a life well-lived and the unique vantage point of an immigrant. Brimming with authentic and genuine experiences viewed through Ravi's indefatigable, positive perspective, it offers a heart-warming and life-affirming manifesto on how to persevere and succeed against all odds. Gentle and purposeful ambition is demonstrated through his unique journey.

Ninan Chacko, corporate executive

Ravi's journey to the United States unfolds through a tapestry of personal and professional trials, showcasing his relentless spirit and resilience. A compelling narrative of overcoming adversity and seizing opportunities, this book is a must-read for anyone inspired by tales of perseverance and triumph.

Kurt Leopoldino, health technology expert

What does it take for an immigrant to succeed in the USA? According to Ravi, it depends on your definition of success. He explains how to achieve self-mastery and equips you with a behavioral blueprint to contribute to the world in your unique way. Through a creative framework called the University of Life, he provides powerful insights to help you deal with failure, stay focused, and make smart life decisions. He has successfully climbed this big, bold mountain and will guide you along the way to face life's challenges and realize your dreams. This is a great read and suitable for anyone on a similar journey.

Chuck Garcia, President, Climb Leadership International and
Professor of Leadership & Professional Development,
Columbia University Graduate School of Engineering,
New York

Ravi Prakash's one-of-a-kind memoir is fascinating and inspiring. It serves up key "life lessons" and professional lessons, connecting a surprising life journey with a truly remarkable professional journey. Nobody else has a story like Ravi's, but he manages to dig down into the universal truths and important lessons we all need for success.

Scot Safon, former Chief Marketing Officer of CNN

Safar is not just a book; it's an immersive journey through the life of an immigrant who defied odds to build a life of meaning and leadership. Prakash's narrative is a tapestry of resilience, adaptation, and triumph against the backdrop of new cultures and challenges. It's a compelling read for anyone seeking inspiration and guidance in navigating life's complexities.

Diego Garcia, Chief Technology Officer at Multiply Sales

A short and relatable story, *Safar* not only takes you through the journey of an immigrant but also delves into life's universal lessons. Ravi Prakash avoids preaching, making it a quick and enjoyable read. With insightful life lessons shared after each chapter, the book provides practical takeaways. It's a narrative that resonates on multiple levels, drawing parallels with everyday challenges we often overlook. A compelling blend of inspiration, relatability, and wisdom extracted from the ordinary grind of life.

Parisha Pandey, young change maker in India

The key ideas found within this book are so valuable and essential for today's society. I think everyone and anyone can learn something from it and will be able to apply it to their own lives. Once I started reading it, I could not stop. It flowed incredibly well—was inspiring and made me want to be a better person. There's nothing more you can ask from a person than this—to become better than who they currently are.

Dr. LeAnne Campbell, Chief Executive Officer, T. Collin
Campbell Center for Nutrition Studies

A compelling narrative that empowers young professionals to harness their inner resilience, conquer challenges, and maximize their potential, reminding readers of the profound impact of making the most out of every circumstance.

Cierra Leopoldo, young professional

This book is inspiring and emotionally evocative for anyone who has recently overcome adversity, is mired in adversity, or who can see adversity on the horizon. Ravi is someone who has walked the walk many times over—anyone could benefit from enjoying this story.

Tom Heagney, young professional

SAFAR

An Immigrant's Journey of Life and Leadership

RAVI PRAKASH

Courageous
Ink

Safar: An Immigrant's Journey of Life and Leadership

Copyright © 2024 by Ravi Prakash
Published by Courageous Ink (Georgia)

Cover by Madelyn Copperwaite of MC Creative LLC
Editing by Jennifer Crosswhite of Tandem Services LLC
Layout by Stephanie Feger of emPower PR Group

First edition, September 2024
ISBN (Paperback): 979-8-9910833-0-0
ISBN (eBook): 979-8-9910833-2-4
ISBN (Hardback): 979-8-9910833-1-7
Library of Congress Control Number: 2024916318
Created in the United States of America

Learn more about Ravi Prakash by visiting www.yoursafar.com. Special discounts are available on quantity book purchases. Contact raviprakash@yoursafar.com for information.

This book is dedicated to my beloved parents, my cherished siblings, my supportive wife, and my two daughters.

It is also for all those kindred spirits who, with unwavering resilience, persist in the face of life's challenges.

Contents

Introduction

*"It's like everyone tells a story about themselves inside their
own head. Always. All the time. That story makes you
what you are. We build ourselves out of that story."*

—Patrick Rothfuss, *The Name of the Wind*

What is it that brings humanity together? What inspires us to open our hearts to those we encounter in life? The answer, in my view, is stories. Stories are the glue that binds and connects us all. We build relationships by telling stories about ourselves and the world around us. It's how we cultivate culture together. How we inspire one another. How we remember. How we pass wisdom down to those who follow in our footsteps. Without storytelling, civilization would cease to exist.

In the pages of this book, you'll find the story of my life's journey to this point, my *safar*, as we say in Hindi, my native tongue. It's no more or less important than your story or the billions of others that have been shared throughout history. But this is a story I take great pride in, one that stands on its own two feet, and I'm sticking to it.

Above all else, this is an immigrant's story—one that millions of expats around the world can likely relate to. I've found a number of common characteristics in the hearts of folks who find success after leaving their homeland in search of a better life. Discipline, determination, diligence, and dedication, to name a few. Living abroad pushes you entirely out of your comfort zone and forces you to develop these traits. It demands that you live in the moment and tackle life's challenges independently. When you have no local support system, there's no plan B to fall back on. You have no choice but to become resourceful. To give up is to fail, a price too high to pay when you're in a foreign country. For expats, resilience becomes second nature.

Of course, you don't need to be an immigrant to access such tenacity for yourself. All of us, regardless of origin, share a similar need to find and fulfill our purpose. We all must navigate the ups and downs of the "University of Life." We pay our entrance fee when we're born, but the graduation requirements are not for the faint of heart. There will always be challenges and lessons to learn. It's my sincere wish that in reading this story, you'll feel inspired to confront the University of Life's tests head on.

Whether or not I've passed those tests myself depends on your definition of the word *success*. I didn't move to the US to get rich or famous, nor to escape the horrors of war. I came because I wanted to prove, both to myself and the world, that I could achieve extraordinary things. I wanted to learn, make the people I cared about proud, and create the best impact I could with whatever life offered me.

These efforts have culminated in a career in leadership, but I never set out to be a leader. Only to live as I am. The desire to fight injustice and stand up for what's right is ingrained in my DNA. While gaining experience navigating the business world, I've sought out roles that allowed me to inspire others to be bold, authentic, and courageous in their own lives. Empowerment is infectious, as is the fulfillment that comes with helping others succeed alongside us.

Leadership, like so many aspects of life, starts from within, it is an inside job. Learning to lead effectively requires us to integrate and personalize the myriad influences of life over time. It involves taking decisive action and making choices that shape us and our future. The doors that opened to me in life only did so after I learned the lessons offered to me by the universe, absorbing that wisdom so I could model it through my actions. We must learn self-mastery first and foremost. If we leave the work of defining who we are to external forces, our dreams of contributing to the world in our own unique way will never come to fruition. It's easy to feel lost, discouraged, or hopeless when life throws curveballs our way. Once we're comfortable in our own skin, however, we open ourselves up to the help, criticism, and failures that allow us to blossom into the person we wish to become. Start within and watch the results of your efforts ripple outward into everything you experience.

"Do not seek outside of yourself."

—Ralph Waldo Emerson

All my life, people have treated me like a container for their assumptions, prejudices, and stereotypes. They find out I'm an immigrant from India and start tossing their labels at me. *Obedient. Works in IT. Hard worker. Arranged marriage?* I didn't fit into America's corporate playbook because while immigrants are viewed as hard workers here, we're also underestimated, taken for granted, and considered unfit for leadership positions. Society expects me to move through life filled to the brim with others' limiting beliefs, carrying the weight of their doubts within me.

Fortunately, my upbringing instilled in me a strong sense of hope. I knew from an early age that if I was going to make it in this chaotic world, I couldn't let my circumstances define me or my potential. I am none of the labels others have tried to assign me. I am not a box made for storing their judgments or ignorance. I'm a whole human being with a place in this universe. We all are. Each of us belongs here.

Life doesn't care who we are or where we come from. There will always be more curveballs waiting for us around the corner. Conquer one mountain, and another will soon present itself. There's never any guarantee that any of us will be here to see the sunrise tomorrow. It's what we do with our time here that defines us. The power to make our world a wonderful place is in our hands. To persevere when the going gets tough, you must have an element of faith rooted in personal experience. From this faith, our efforts can blossom and bear fruit.

I've led many hardworking teams of up to 1,000 people from over eighty countries on multimillion to multibillion-dollar IT projects. I've traveled the world, run several marathons, founded a cricket club, and taught workshops on the benefits of plant-based nutrition. I'm a husband and father of a beautiful family that lights up my life, but this blissful status quo wasn't easy to create. Achieving all this took decades of struggle and grit.

In truth, I was a middle-class kid from India, at one point blind in one eye, who went completely broke on more than one occasion as an adult. When I was a teenager, my teachers doubted I'd even graduate from high school, let alone end up in the US with three master's degrees. But I kept making decisions that would move me forward regardless of whatever outcome I might reach. This decision-making habit has done more for me than any specific goal I could set for myself.

My unconventional trajectory began with a somewhat unconventional childhood. I was fortunate to grow up in India surrounded by those who had fought for our independence following 200 years of imperial British rule. As a citizen of a young democratic nation trying to find its footing in the world, I knew I had to walk my path with my eyes wide open.

That's where my journey began, so let us begin there.

ONE

Sowing the Seeds

"You can't connect the dots looking forward. You can only connect them looking backward."

—Steve Jobs

I've been a fighter from the moment I was born but was nearly robbed of my chance to be a part of this world in the first place. It's a miracle, if you believe in such things, that I was even allowed to take a single breath. Two days before my birth, my mother was involved in a bloody car wreck that drove an iron rod through her skull. Blood flowed from the wound like water from a faucet until doctors at a nearby hospital were able to save her. Though she survived, there was fear I would not.

When I was finally born, my body was blue due to a lack of oxygen in my blood. But I made it through those crucial first moments, stabilizing enough to safely head home with my mother, who also made a full recovery. As I would eventually come to understand, resilience and tenacity have long run in our family. Together with Mom, my father, and three older sisters, I was allowed to embark on this adventure we call life, daring it to show me what else it had.

"It takes a village to raise a child," they say, and I may as well be the poster child for that expression.

I credit much of my resilience during my formative years to the lively environment I grew up in and the cast of characters involved. We all move through life connected to everyone around us, and the events of our childhoods lay the foundation for who we go on to become. Along my journey, there have been numerous *inflection points*—occurrences big and small that changed the trajectory of my thinking, beliefs, values, decisions, and actions—which I've only been able to fully appreciate in hindsight. It's these moments that pull us forward, guiding us toward our fate.

I was born in India during the 1960s to a family rooted in an expansive web of community. During summers at my paternal grandparents' house when I was a boy, we would often have the entire village of Tilakpur over, filling their courtyard in the evenings.

Tilakpur was named after the legendary Tilka Majhi, a local fisherman who refused to pay taxes to the British and took up arms against them in 1784. That event, as I was told, sparked the beginning of India's nationwide movement for freedom from British rule. The buzz of revolution still danced in the air there.

On those nights, five hundred cups of tea would be served and passed around in that courtyard as guests of all ages mingled, danced, laughed, sang, cried, and talked through life's ups and downs. This wasn't a culture my grandparents created, or even the culture of our village, specifically. The mood reflected the greater culture of India at the time.

It just so happened that in our village, our house, was the center of gravity.

It was in this environment that I first learned the value of stories.

Ravi with his grandpa, sisters and cousins

Ravi's ancestral home in Tilakpur

On those balmy nights with the waters of the Ganges flowing nearby, people had all kinds of interesting conversations. Talk of recipes, politics, weather, crops, cost of living, education, health issues. But the way those conversations were told, through storytelling, was most significant. We would sit in circles, sometimes hopping from one to another, listening intently, eager to share and learn about our history as it was unfolding. On some nights, the sky was pitch black, with only the stars to illuminate its expansive void. Hearing the stories of the village gave us all a feeling of boundlessness, as if we were as limitless as the infinite universe above. We felt the magic of life and all its possibilities rushing through us. These moments surpassed the transactional nature of everyday connection and, over time, tied us together in love.

I don't suspect most children get to hear such a wide range of topics discussed from a young age, but I didn't think much of it at the time. All I knew was that I loved to listen. The words of those around me seeped into my mind and caused me to daydream. I began to imagine who I might become later in life. What I could or couldn't do. Where I might go. Whether I'd be able to travel and see the world like the brave people my sisters and I heard about on those nights. If I could achieve even a tenth of what the people around me had done, at least that would be *something*.

To live, age, and die passively would never be enough to satisfy the hunger my community instilled in me as a boy. The seeds of my calling were planted by those stories—a calling to do something different. Something big.

The string of decades before I was born had been socially and politically volatile, culminating in India's independence from British rule in 1947. We didn't lack examples of heroism in our culture. Mahatma Gandhi, Khan Abdul Ghaffar Khan (known as Frontier Gandhi), Prime Minister Jawaharlal Nehru, and President Rajendra Prasad were just a handful of my grandparents' friends and contemporaries. Those times had touched them personally and were still fresh in their minds when I was a boy.

My paternal grandparents were well-known freedom fighters who had spent their lives leading the resistance against the British Raj. To hear of their courageous actions gave me a deep sense of connection to my country and our freshly won independence. I was lucky enough to attend multiple political gatherings with them as a kid. I couldn't understand everything that was discussed there, but the stories I heard left me in awe.

Ravi's grandpa with the first Prime Minister of India

My grandfather, Siya Ram Singh, had been wanted dead or alive by the British throughout his life, fighting with a bounty of twenty million rupees on his head at one point. He'd hidden in sewers to escape their clutches and pretended to be insane whenever he was caught, leading them to assume they'd caught the wrong man and should set him free. Winston Churchill was so concerned about his activities that he dubbed him the Tiger of Bihar. In spite of it all, my grandfather ended up accomplishing much in the way of influencing others to support the movement for freedom. People far and wide adored him for his mind, heart, and efforts. He was the ultimate example of leadership through the lens of love, courage, and integrity.

Ravi's grandpa with first and future second Prime Minister of India

Ravi's paternal grandparents

Ravi's maternal grandparents

Grandma Saraswati Devi, my father's mother, had an equally important role in creating opportunities people of India still enjoy today. She ran a huge agriculture business and served as one of the founding members of the first college for women in the city of Patna. Despite never formally attending school herself, she'd been instrumental in advancing local women's rights and education. She also served on our state legislature and was a force to be reckoned with when she spoke at political meetings, commanding the attention of listeners far and wide.

While my paternal grandparents served as potent role models in the area of political leadership, my maternal grandparents complemented their efforts through economic leadership.

We spent every single winter with my mom's parents in the village of Pandaul where they lived. My mom's dad, the late Jagat Narayan Sharma, founded a handspun cotton and silk business. Though he lacked any formal education, he established retail locations in four cities— Bombay, Calcutta, Banaras, and

Patna. He sent his four brothers to manage the shops while he operated the business from a small village in eastern India near the Nepalese border.

As a child looking up to him, he seemed infinitely rich to me, but what I admired most about him was his work ethic. He was always punctual and dressed to impress in traditional white cotton clothing ironed with starch. His shops looked immaculate. Everything had its place. He was also a wonderful cook and dazzled everyone with his neat English handwriting, which I greatly admired at the time. Talented, smart, and decisive, he wowed everyone around him.

My maternal grandmother, the late Sonamati Sharma, was somewhat underestimated by other people but served as the backbone of the family. Even as a kid, I could sense that the main energy and drive of the household started with her. She, like my other grandma, never received formal education, but stood firm as the voice of reason—a symbol of vision, patience, and courage. Articulate and persuasive, she would quietly influence family decisions. In the years that followed my grandfather's death, she encouraged my sisters and me to seek out advanced education and create our own path despite the fact that women were still pressured to be homemakers in those days. She died shortly after I got married but managed to make it to my wedding and met my Brazilian wife. Though they couldn't speak each other's languages, my grandma's gaze and warm hug conveyed her deep love and willingness to welcome my wife into our family. She was one of the most open-minded people I've ever known.

Many of the qualities I saw in all four of my grandparents were direct results of their generation's values.

I admired and respected their integrity and courage, even when I disagreed with their ideas. After all the atrocities they had endured during the British Raj, none of them were bitter or jaded about the world. They remained focused on inspiring determination and self-reliance in the hearts of Indian citizens. They seemed highly driven and, at the same time, oddly content.

"A happy person is not a person in a certain set of circum-stances but rather a person with a certain set of attitudes."

—Hugh Downs, broadcaster and host

Descended from those four heroes were my caring but very matter-of-fact parents. My dad, Rajendra Prasad Singh, was an executive working in marketing and sales. The freedom-fighter lifestyle of my paternal grandparents had required him and his siblings to essentially raise themselves while their parents were out tussling with the British at protests, though they always knew they were loved.

Every morning throughout my childhood, he would wake up at four a.m. to buy milk from the local dairy before starting his day of calls with people all over the country. He had the memory of an elephant, able to rattle off complex mental math and hundreds of phone numbers without looking up a single digit. He was always dedicated, punctual, and well dressed. He was also a jokester, loved writing poems, and was a master of public speaking. When anyone he knew was in need, he'd connect the dots to help them, especially those who were unemployed.

Hearing his stories at the dinner table influenced how I'd go on to process the good, the bad, and the ugly of work culture.

His job was stressful, and many of his business peers were less than honest in their daily lives, dealing in bribes and shady favors. Dad did everything by the book, careful never to cut corners, and always carried himself with integrity, even with a high personal cost.

My mom, Anuradha Singh, was a housewife with five kids—my four sisters and myself—and raised us without help from any of the modern amenities we take for granted today, like ovens, dishwashers, and food processors. All she had to work with was a gas stove. Her cooking was (and still is) legendary. Every meal we ate was fresh and made from scratch, including her salads, spiced rice, lentils, chutney, and roti. We never went hungry or wore clothes that weren't clean and ironed, as Mom was always on top of it.

Ravi's mother and father

She's also one of the best communicators I've ever known, able to talk about difficult issues in ways that allow others to calm down and consider alternative perspectives. After cooking and helping us kids get ready in the morning, she would have friends over to chat, knit, and drink tea out in our garden. Thanks to her approach to life and relationships, my parents enjoyed the best marriage I've witnessed thus far. They disagreed at times but never argued, and our house was filled with the peace of their example.

Ravi with his parents and siblings

There were five kids in our family, with me being the fourth and the only boy. My oldest sister, Rajni, spent much of her childhood living with my mom's parents before majoring in literature and entering the business world. My second oldest sister, Rashmi, was athletic, somewhat mischievous, and always in good spirits. Shabnam, the sister before me, was incredibly smart and driven from a young age. She would go on to study zoology, work as a teacher and lawyer, and get involved in politics. Archana, my younger sister, was a dreamer who wanted to become an actress and future prime minister as a kid. She went on to study computer programming, teach yoga, and become an author. (I guess writing runs in the family!)

When they weren't working, my parents were fun-loving people who liked to travel. They took me and my sisters to many places, and our home never lacked guests. Every evening, someone either came to our house for tea or we went to theirs. On weekends, tea became lunch or dinner. Aunts, uncles, cousins, and friends were always accessible and present. With so much activity percolating around us, my sisters and I were able to find ourselves and were encouraged to stand on our own two feet.

Sometimes people asked my parents why they encouraged their four daughters to go to college when they would likely just go on to marry and become housewives, anyway. Their answer was that we were all their children, equally capable and deserving of the security of an independent life, and denying any of us an education wasn't an option in their minds.

They wanted whatever might be best for us in the future.

Our summers and winters were spent with my grandparents in Tilakpur and Pandaul; my immediate family and I lived in the desert city of Jodhpur during my earliest years. Known for its sky-blue buildings and military bases, Jodhpur lay some 120 kilometers east of the border of Pakistan.

When the Indo-Pakistani war was declared on December 3, 1971, our local army and air force service members were called to arms, and the area became an active war zone. I remember the initial excitement bubbling among the kids at school when the war was declared. Our final exams were coming up but had to be postponed due to the fighting. At one point, the government ordered us to move to the trenches for nearly two weeks, as we were less likely to be killed by the bombings there than we would have been in our concrete homes. We helped dig those trenches, covered them in greenery, and remained there, aside from when the sirens blared to signal it was safe to fetch food and water from outside. We would huddle together, listening to our shortwave radio for news about what was happening around us.

At night, we would leave the lights out in the trenches, as any light would make us a target for the Pakistani soldiers, and watch the dark sky light up above us with blasts from their jets. I watched smoke billow from a raging fire at an army containment center close to my house after it was bombed.

When the war finally ended and we began heading back to school, we were delayed by the return of the service members who had been fighting at the border. People lined the streets in gratitude, throwing flowers in their path. I didn't overanalyze or fully appreciate the gravity of that situation, but I was disturbed by the suffering of those involved. People had lost their eyes, arms, and legs in battle. Mothers and fathers lost the children they'd raised to adulthood. Tension grew in my heart after witnessing some of the horrors we human beings are capable of.

Why do we have to do this to each other?

But with that tension grew a sense of curiosity about the world and the various things that might be happening in far-off lands. My dad had a boss during those years who traveled internationally. I didn't know where he went or what he did while he was away, but I always admired how he spoke and carried himself. There was an air of world-liness permeating his aura, and he left me with the impression that people who explored the world were intelligent, capable, and exciting. I had grown up listening to epic stories, after all, and travelers like him always had incredible stories to tell. At that point, I had no desire to leave India, but I understood that beyond the horizon, the world offered more than just the terror of war.

My father's job involved being transferred often, requiring our family to move frequently. In 1972, we left Jodhpur for Kolkata, spelled Calcutta at the time. We weren't there for more than a year, but I remember it well due to the liveliness of the place. The former capital, known today for its grand colonial architecture, art galleries, and festivals, was a boisterous and somewhat dangerous place. Sociopolitical unrest permeated the local culture due to rampant unemployment, labor disputes, and rising violent crime.

Though my family was always middle class, rent in Calcutta was more expensive than in Jodhpur, and our living situation reflected the shift. We moved into a one-room apartment in a high-rise building there, which we divided into small areas with curtains for privacy. Dad traveled nonstop for work that year, leaving for weeks at a time so he could make his way up the ladder in his sales career. This meant my mom was often alone with the five of us, making it an especially hard year for her. On top of the cooking, cleaning, laundry, and childcare, she essentially became a live-in nurse as well. We lived next to a dump where people dropped their garbage, and we were constantly getting sick from breathing the dirty air.

As we settled into our new arrangement, my parents searched for schools we kids could attend in the area, but it was difficult to find any that would admit children from families that moved all the time. My sisters got into one fairly close to our home, but the one I was accepted to was located three hours away on foot. Six days a week, a chaperone would arrive at four a.m. to walk me to school. We would arrive at 7:00 a.m., study until four p.m., and walk three hours home. Then I'd shower, eat, finish my homework, and get to bed so I could repeat the process all over again the next day. Walking long distances to and from school isn't uncommon in developing countries, even to this day, and this was the only choice available to us at the time.

I never complained about getting up early, as everyone was used to it in my house. My father insisted we all become early risers. In Hindi there's a saying similar to the one about the early bird and the worm in

English: "It's early morning. Those who sleep will lose. Those who wake up will gain." Every time my father said it, the words pierced through our hearts, conditioning us to seize the day and make the most of every opportunity.

During that walk to and from school each day, I would pass homeless families on the street living in dire poverty. We didn't interact much, and no one ever asked me for anything. They would simply smile with kindness or make small comments, aware I was on my way to school. I was only in third grade but knew those children weren't offered the same opportunity for an education that I was. I felt the privilege in my little heart, though I did not have the words to describe it.

I learned to be cautious during that year, as Calcutta had been rife with kidnappings in those days. One Saturday afternoon, my chaperone was delayed for several hours after school, and I had to wait for him outside, alone and desperately hungry. Unbeknownst to me, my mother got worried and called a cousin who attended the same school, asking him to find me. Just before he arrived, a strange man approached me, asking whether I was hungry and offering to take me to eat dosa, my favorite dish, at a restaurant. I accepted, naïve about his intentions. As my mom's cousin rounded the corner and spotted me, the man quickly disappeared. Everyone in our family was told what happened. The adults feared that had those few moments unfolded differently, I would likely have been taken and never seen again.

In spite of our hardships, my family's year in Calcutta was filled with bright moments.

There's a festival there each year where people celebrate Vishvakarma, the architect of the gods, regarded as the patron deity of all craftspeople. On that day, everyone in the city flies kites, filling the sky with the sight of them. The kite strings are laced with fine pieces of glass, which we used to cut each other's strings and see how many kites we could collect as a game.

One of my sisters and I were on the terrace of our apartment complex and spotted a kite stuck at the top of a steep water tank that supplied water to the neighborhood. Together, we climbed to the top to collect the kite, risking death in the process. If we'd slipped, we'd have fallen to the street, but we didn't care. Our determination fueled us. We got in trouble when a neighbor spotted us but felt it was worth it when we got home and beheld our bounty. We'd collected over a hundred kites that day and looked forward to flying them all in the days to come. When we finally left Calcutta, however, the kites were forgotten during the move. All our hard work wasted! At the time, it felt like a great loss.

Looking back, I now believe life was giving my sisters and me a chance to develop good habits and self-discipline that year, aided by the guidance of our parents, neighbors, and teachers.

Our lifestyle gave us a sense of the contrast; Calcutta and Jodhpur were like night and day. Everywhere we went in Calcutta, we'd hear music emanating from homes. It was one of the best-educated cities in the world at the time.

By the time we moved again, we were very ready to leave, but our year there had brought us closer as a family. We had become stronger, able to adjust to hard circumstances together. We'd found comfort in discomfort, and I carried that skill forward as part of the foundation on which I stand today.

In 1973, my dad got transferred again, and we moved to the town of Sindri, home to the biggest fertilizer plant in Asia and the very first industrial complex India built after gaining its independence. Nearly everyone in town worked for the plant, which meant everyone knew each other. The neighborhoods were well planned, dotted with schools and playgrounds, so I no longer had to walk three hours to and from school each way. My family got to move into a nice house with a big backyard and plenty of space to host guests. Nearby, a ring road surrounded a park where families could play and throw parties. The environment in Sindri felt more like an intimate village than a town, infinitely more peaceful than the hectic bustle of Calcutta, and we made ourselves at home there, staying all the way through my tenth-grade year.

Two of the best things about our neighbors in Sindri were their wealth of knowledge and their desire to help each other.

The people hired to work at the plant were well educated and there was also an esteemed engineering college located nearby. My sisters and I could always go to someone for help with our studies. One could teach us math, another could help with physics, chemistry, English, or economics. They knew it all, and throughout this process of learning, my family got to know all of their families.

Birthday parties at our house were like festivals, growing in size as the years went by. We would close off the road, set up a huge tent, and have the whole town join us in celebration. Thousands of people came, which meant my parents and neighbors had to spend quite a lot of time cooking in our backyard. No one focused on barriers like class, religion, or language, and few people ever spoke badly of each other. It was through those interactions that I started to understand the importance of human relationships. We not only cared for each other but knew what might happen to our little town if we didn't. It had only been twenty-six years since India gained independence, and without the cooperation of everyone in the community, places like Sindri would never have been able to develop into the economically robust areas we see today.

My father drew attention to our family once his passion for helping those less fortunate became known to those in the area. There was an engineering college close to our house. Students would come and go, and Dad would often invite them over to help them find jobs. He would introduce them to businesspeople in their industries of interest, never expecting anything in return, opening new doors for them out of the goodness of his heart. People all through town would speak well of him.

"Ah! You're Ravi! Your father is the only truly honest man I ever met." I could only hope people would speak of me the same way someday.

One day in Sindri, I had an experience that changed the way I would view life forever. My dad had a motorized scooter he would ride around town. I had always wanted to drive it, begging him for years. Finally, when I was in seventh grade, he gave me permission. Thrilled, I hopped on it immediately, driving fast around the ring road that circled the neighborhood. Rounding one of the corners on the way back to my house, I failed to slow down in time and crashed the bike with a loud *BANG!* Neighbors poured into the street to see what had caused the commotion, rushing over to see if I was hurt.

My father walked over, hands folded, and waved them off. "Don't touch him."

I looked up at him, dusting myself off and checking the scrapes on my skin, wondering whether he was angry with me.

"Get back on the scooter," he said firmly, "and take another round."

I was shocked by his command, already deciding to never drive another scooter for the rest of my days. I didn't argue, however. Carefully, in front of a neighborhood of onlookers, I mounted the scooter once more and started driving. This time, it was different. I knew the curve of the road and how much I needed to slow down to round each corner safely. Focused but relaxed, I felt the wind rush across my skin and through my hair. An inner freedom blossomed in that moment, and all the fear I had just felt turned to triumph. Victorious, I completed the loop, arriving to applause from the neighbors. A look of pride stretched across my father's face, and I absorbed his faith in me as my own.

"The only way to escape from the prison of fear is action."

—Joe Tye, author and Chief Executive Officer of Values Coach Inc.

My memory of that day didn't coalesce around the accomplishment of riding a scooter without crashing. It was about the way my father had helped me remove fear from my emotional vocabulary. I could have headed back inside to tend to my bruises in defeat. I could've filed away the accident as an embarrassing source of trauma, but I didn't. With Dad's guidance, I internalized that "failure" as a major inflection point in my life.

Thanks to the accident that day, I not only developed valuable skills in defensive driving, but also an *element of faith.*

I saw that no matter what happened during my life, I'd come out the other side (if the experience didn't kill me) and be able to reach even higher heights with courage and wisdom under my feet. Our fear is the enemy, not our mistakes, and by persevering in spite of it, we become our own heroes.

My determination to do something extraordinary in life was fortified that day, a feeling that crossed over into my sports interests more than my education. I hadn't been a particularly good student. The problem wasn't that I was stupid or incapable. For me, the issue was that I didn't find my teachers interesting enough to capture my imagination. Teachers—who reflected society at large—were mostly interested in grades. I was interested in testing my physical limits and questioned the conventional path of becoming a doctor or engineer. I, like millions of kids in India, was more interested in playing sports professionally, especially cricket. Playing cricket in the big leagues was the dream.

The conventional wisdom in India at the time, however, was that you had to study academics hard, or you'd never amount to anything in life. By the time I entered tenth grade, the teachers at my school had a bet as to whether or not I'd graduate. Many assumed I'd be held back or drop out altogether. Mr. Basu, an exceptional English teacher who actually managed to capture my imagination at school, promised me a set of Parker Pens, a very prized item in India when I was growing up, if I passed.

As luck would have it, pass I did, and before graduation day, a guest speaker came to our school who reinforced my curiosity about the world. He had ridden through sixty-nine countries on his bicycle. I was in awe as he spoke, mesmerized by his athleticism, wondering if I could ever get to his level of endurance.

Would I ever be able to travel and go places in life like he did?

I got the same feeling listening to him that I had while reading about the exploits of Edmond Hillary and Tenzing Norgay, and while listening to my dad's boss, the late SN Sharma. My desire to prove my worth to the world—and to myself—took up more and more space in my consciousness.

After tenth grade was over, my dad got transferred and we moved again, this time to the capital city of New Delhi. Before we left Sindri, we were invited to hundreds (yes, hundreds!) of meals with families all over town and didn't cook anything at home for six months. We were sad to leave behind our friends and the wonderful memories we had made at that place. It would take over a year to make it to the homes of everyone who had invited us, but we didn't have enough time as a family, and eventually the responsibility to tie up loose ends fell on my dad. Whenever Dad visited Sindri on business trips, he had several standing invitations to attend for breakfast, lunch, and dinner.

I traveled ahead of my family in the cargo truck with all our belongings, eager to show I could handle important family responsibilities as a teenager. (I was also getting tired of the endless farewell parties, if I'm honest, and happy to have an excuse to decline.) The journey should have only taken two days but took three and a half because the movers and I ran into a mechanical issue in Uttar Pradesh. They froze, panicked that we had broken down in the middle of nowhere, not knowing where or how to get help. I came up with an idea.

"Go to the nearest village," I told them, "and ask if there are any fertilizer dealers who buy fertilizer from my dad's company."

As luck would have it, there was one nearby. Upon hearing my father's name and learning who I was, the man sprung into action and got us help, all thanks to Dad's reputation. He told me that if it were anyone else, he wouldn't have bothered to help us. Again, looking back, it seems like the universe was sending a message to me about how to carry myself.

Integrity matters and can get you far, especially when you're in a bind.

Our new home in New Delhi was an apartment on the second floor of a building lined with shops on the ground level. You name it; they sold it down there. Clothes, jewelry, juice, toys, furniture. The varied commerce of the area attracted traffic and pedestrians to our street all day, making it loud and busy from morning till night. When the rest of my family arrived, we focused on settling in once more. *My* main focus, however, was cricket.

This is where I'll make it big, I thought. *I'll play here and make it onto the Indian cricket team. Finally, I'll be able to start my career.*

Soon after our arrival, my dad walked with me to the local government high school to enroll me in my courses. The principal was a retired army colonel who kept a long bamboo cane on his desk. Corporal punishment was (and still is) common in India, so I knew that weapon wasn't there for show. He sat across from me and my father and asked me what I wanted to study. My three options were arts, commerce, or science.

Now, back at home before the meeting, I had told my parents science would be my choice. In reality, I'd had no intention of following through with that idea. In my mind, I wanted to have time to play cricket and specializing in science would take way too much effort. That day in the principal's office, I told him I wanted to study the arts. It didn't even take five seconds for my father to stand and walk out of the room in disappointment. He went home and told my mother in anger that their only son would never amount to anything in life.

I began my arts courses and within two days was bored to death. Without telling my parents, I went back to the principal and told him I wanted to study commerce. "That's fine," he told me, and reenrolled me in the commerce program.

A few days later, I was bored to death again, wanting nothing to do with any of those classes. I returned to the principal's office once more to tell him it wasn't working out. I wanted to study science. By that point, he'd grown annoyed with my ambivalence.

"Look," he said, "I have one spot left in the science department that two other students are competing for. You'll have to take an exam, and if you pass with the highest score, you can switch. If not, you'll continue in commerce. Understood?"

I accepted his challenge, studied as hard as I could, and was able to pass the exam with flying colors. Upon entering the science program, I started excelling in school for the first time in my life, but this wasn't solely a result of my desire for success. The standard of the school was rooted in the principal's outlook on life. He told us that if you studied science in India and graduated with a score of less than ninety-five percent, you'd have no future. The country was simply too competitive. We either had to do exceedingly well or fail altogether. There was no gray area.

As expected, the demanding nature of my studies left me with little to no time to play cricket outside of school. At some point, however, I convinced my dad to take me to the grounds of the Delhi Cricket Association in Firoza Kotla, where the professionals would play. I met a coach there who signed me up to play on an amateur team, which I did for several months. My dreams of international glory became more deeply entrenched in my mind. I was practicing on the same grounds that produced some of India's greatest pros. One of my amateur teammates, Sanjeev Sharma, went on to play for the national team and I was sure to follow in his footsteps. In my mind, everything was unfolding according to plan. I'd graduate from high school, become a professional cricket star, and be able to take pride in being the admirable man I'd always wanted to be.

Until one day in twelfth grade when the unthinkable happened: I suddenly lost all sight in my right eye. In an instant, everything went dark.

I rushed to the doctor after school for a diagnosis, and after conducting a few tests, the specialists there told me they'd have to patch my good eye up. Hearing those words felt like a kick to the chest. I imagined being blind forever, unable to accomplish any of the big dreams in my heart. Returning home from the hospital, I lost all hope for my future, hitting the lowest point of my entire life up to that point. How would I ever play cricket? How would I even graduate if I couldn't see?

After I told my family what was happening, my dad took me back to the hospital. The doctor explained that my right eye was completely blind due to a nerve issue, but my left eye still had 20/20 vision. By patching up my good eye, the bad eye would be forced to work harder, and I might be able to retain some of my eyesight by rebuilding those muscles. My condition, they surmised, might have resulted as a side effect of the car accident my mother got into just before my birth. The doctors had mentioned a slight injury to my eyes while talking to my parents in the hospital but didn't think much of the damage, given that I was an otherwise healthy newborn.

Initially, I couldn't see anything. My world was pitch black, and I needed help doing the most basic of tasks. Shabnam, the sister closest to me in age, was in twelfth grade at the same time I was and had to help me study each day. Gradually, my eyesight improved to the point where I could see a little better. With great effort and support from my sister, parents, and teachers, I was able to graduate on time (though not with the score of ninety-five percent I was told I would need for success).

With my eye treatment still ongoing, however, I had to forgo a year of progress, leaving me stuck at home figuring out how to handle my future while all my friends went off to college. Playing cricket professionally was obviously off the table with my visual impairment. I'd have to let go of that lifelong dream and come up with another plan but had no idea what to do. How would I ever find the passion I'd had for cricket elsewhere?

What's an athlete without the game?

One afternoon during this period of existential crisis, a bunch of relatives came to our family's house to visit as usual. My sister and I were waiting for the results of our twelfth grade national board exam, which would determine what kind of college we'd each be able to attend. We sat with everyone in the living room talking about what we wanted to do in the future. My sister wanted to become a doctor, like many students in India at the time. Truth be told, she was whip smart and entirely capable of achieving her goal.

I, by contrast, still wasn't sure what I wanted to do next, though I'd been thinking about studying agriculture. I was always a rebel of sorts and had no interest in pursuing what others expected of me, and nutrition had been important to me as an athlete. Perhaps I could become a specialist in healthy eating. I could envision that a young country like India with a rapidly growing population would need experts to help feed the masses efficiently.

Upon hearing our dreams for the future, a brother-in-law of mine who worked at the Russian embassy in New Delhi spoke up. He was a street-smart guy who was proud of his job, and I had always liked him as a kid. That day, he told my sister and me about a program that sponsored 400 Indian students to study in Russia each year, all expenses paid. My sister and I had never heard of such an opportunity. We'd never thought such a thing could even be possible. My sister listened to him with stars in her eyes, interested in the program and how it worked, wondering whether she might actually be able to study abroad for free.

As we listened and asked questions, my brother-in-law's expression turned into one of doubt. Eyeing us with skepticism, he said he might be able to put in a good word for us with the embassy but didn't think either of us would be able to go anywhere without his help. I had never expressed any interest in studying abroad, but the way he said those words in front of our family sparked a fire in me that would go on to change my life forever. Had he been joking, I'd have been able to brush it off, but the feeling underlying his tone was one of condescension. He hadn't intended to be harsh or insulting, but I could tell he had no faith in our abilities. In his eyes, we didn't have the knowledge, skills, or money to make our way in the world without someone else pulling strings for us along the way. I didn't respond to his words, nor did anyone else in the room. The moment passed unnoticed by everyone but me, but it got under my skin. It just did.

All my life, people had underestimated me. I'd been a subpar student raised by a family of heroes who had helped spark a revolution. My parents and teachers were all less than enthusiastic about my future prospects. There I was with a patch over my left eye, a year behind in my education, robbed of my dream of becoming a cricket star despite being a great player. And there he was, a member of my own family who I respected, reinforcing my fear in front of everyone I cared about that I would never amount to anything. I would always have to depend on others and follow in their footsteps rather than forging my own path, according to him. The thought of it silently drove me nuts.

We often assume something monumental has to take place in our lives for a major breakthrough to occur.

Most of the time, however, our lives are transformed by small, seemingly insignificant moments. This was one of those moments for me. Another unexpected inflection point. I simply couldn't let it go. The doubt in my brother-in-law's voice was the last straw. The time had come to get serious, harden my determination, and take control of my own destiny.

I would prove to myself I could succeed in the world.

I'd show my brother-in-law.

I'd show my family and my teachers.

I'd show every friend and classmate who'd gone off to college before me.

I'd show everyone.

University of Life

LESSON #1: INFLECTION POINTS

Inflection points are the potentially transformative moments of our lives. Often modest and seemingly insignificant, they change our trajectory as they pass by. Shifting, we move forward, pulled by the future that awaits us. Taking time to reflect enables us to identify these moments and follow their lead. What have been some powerful inflection points in your life?

TWO

The Pull of the World

"A journey of a thousand miles begins with a single step."

—Chinese Proverb

The morning after the vexing conversation with my brother-in-law, I woke up early as always and got dressed for the day. It was the middle of summer, terribly hot and humid, but I wasn't about to let the weather stop me. I took my cotton bag and told Mom, "I'm going out. I'll be back."

"Where are you off to, Ravi?"

"I'll tell you later."

I was suddenly intensely focused on the goal of traveling somehow, just as I had dreamed of doing since I was a young boy listening to the stories of my grandparents. This gnawing desire had nothing to do with studying in Russia or anywhere in particular. It came down to a yearning to embrace adventure and discover the unknown. I would become worldly, knowledgeable, and self-sufficient, like my dad and his boss. Like the speaker at my school in Sindri who had ridden his bicycle through sixty-nine countries on his own. Since I had finally learned to accept that I would never become a professional cricket player, it was time to see if I could make some traveling dreams come true.

I headed by bus to the area of New Delhi where the consulates and embassies are located. I didn't have a game plan or speak much English at the time. I just started knocking on doors, doing whatever I could to talk with the counselors who worked for foreign governments. Day after day I went back, hopping from consulate to consulate to gather information about my prospects. Security there was nothing like it is these days. Pretty much every employee I spoke with let me in and helpfully tried to point me in the right direction. Finally, a man at the American embassy advised me to visit the US Education Foundation office, which was located in a different area of the city.

When I finally got there and knocked on the door, they invited me in to speak with a kind woman from the States who reminded me of my grandma. She walked me out to a garden area on the property, and we sat on a bench swing.

There, we talked for hours about my dreams for the future and what life was like in the US. She was clearly interested in helping me however she could.

By the end of the conversation, she had explained that if I wanted to go abroad, I would have to get my undergraduate degree in India, which I would need to apply for graduate school in the US, along with enough money to guarantee my survival there.

There was no way I'd be able to gather the thousands of dollars I would need to make my way in America at that point. Not without help from my family, at least, which I wasn't willing to ask for after my brother-in-law's condescending comment. I thanked the woman from the education office for her time and left, now aware of what I would need to make this new dream a reality.

I never shared my intention of going to the US with anyone. I locked the advice from the woman in the depths of my soul with steely resolve, and it stayed there, silently guiding my journey as I searched for an undergraduate program that would move me forward.

After a year of applying to colleges while my right eye got stronger, I was finally accepted to the University of Agricultural Sciences in Bangalore, down in the southern part of India. On October 31, 1984, as I was in the process of preparing to leave, I headed to the All-India Institute of Medical Sciences in New Delhi for my final eye checkup. It was clear from the moment I arrived at the hospital that something terrible had happened. The building was packed with police and army personnel, signaling someone important had likely been brought there.

Sensing that trouble might be brewing in the city, I took the first bus home. There, I heard the news that Prime Minister Indira Gandhi had been assassinated that morning by her bodyguards, both Sikh nationalists.

The period leading up to the event had been marked by increasing tension between the Indian government and Sikh separatists demanding an independent state of their own, which they called Khalistan. Prime Minister Gandhi had ordered Operation Blue Star, an Indian Army mission to remove militant Sikh terrorists who had taken refuge in the Golden Temple complex in Amritsar, a city in the north-western state of Punjab. The operation was aimed at flushing out Jarnail Singh Bhindranwale, the leading figure of the Khalistan movement, and his armed supporters. By the time all was said and done, significant damage had been done to the Golden Temple and many civilians had been killed throughout the city, causing outrage among Sikhs nationwide.

When Indira Gandhi's bodyguards assassinated her in retaliation, fierce and immediate political instability ensued, particularly in India's capital, where my family and I lived. Rumors of all kinds began spreading among politicians and the public about what would happen next. Tension had been rising in the region for far too long and certain groups were ready to take matters into their own hands.

The neighborhood where my family and I lived was made up primarily of Sikh families who owned local businesses, many of whom had moved to New Delhi after fleeing Pakistan, which would become Muslim-controlled, during the Indo-Pakistani war. The Sikhs we knew were loving, hardworking people who had lived alongside us in harmony. Many of the older folks talked out in the street that day, shaking and sobbing in fear, reminded of the war that had plagued the western area of our country in August 1947, when India was divided into Pakistan and India. No one wanted to see more violence.

Sensing the gravity of the situation, my father first briefed us as a family, then called on our neighbors and friends to bring everyone in the neighborhood into the street for a matter-of-fact conversation.

We went knocking on doors, inviting families and business owners to join us. Once we had all gathered, Dad explained that the situation in the city was so unstable, we all could lose everything tomorrow. Only 300 kilometers lay between New Delhi and Punjab, where the Sikh separatists had focused their activities, and supporters of their terrorism lived throughout the region, especially there in the capital.

There would also be anger from Hindus and supporters of Prime Minister Gandhi seeking revenge, along with clashes from political dissidents. Should any mob come marching down our block, we would have to protect each other and work together to deal with the situation as it unfolded. The worst thing we could do, Dad told us, would be to provoke violence in our own neighborhood. Everyone listened and nodded with nothing to add but agreement, sharing his desire to keep things peaceful.

That evening, chaos descended upon the city. New Delhi was awash with riots, looting, and civil unrest. We all tossed and turned in bed, wide awake, waiting in fear of what would come. Early that morning, Dad told us all to put on a couple layers of clothing in case our house was looted. We gathered our important paperwork and the bit of money Dad had put aside for me to take to college in Bangalore. At around 7:00 a.m., the din of a large crowd began growing in the distance. Angry voices, chanting, and the sound of breaking glass echoed through the streets.

Together with our neighbors, we ran up to the terrace on the fourth floor of our apartment building and looked out over the city. The skyline was streaked with clouds of smoke. The sound of the crowd grew louder and was clearly moving fast, coming right for our area. Within minutes, thousands of people came walking along the main road of our neighborhood, smashing and burning down anything in their path.

Terrified, we ran back into the building, panicking over how to protect ourselves and our homes. When the mob turned the corner and came walking down our block, my father did the unthinkable.

He went outside, stood in the middle of the street, and yelled at the crowd to stop the destruction. Shaking, my family and I looked on from inside, watching as a few people pelted him with stones. He stood his ground, blocking their way with the blood of his revolutionist parents coursing through his veins.

"Move another inch forward, and you'll have to walk over my dead body!"

Right at that moment, the son of our landlord, who had been a classmate of mine, ran into the street holding a sword with his head held high. My father slapped him and shoved him back into our building, desperate not to provoke the mob any further or give them an excuse to harm us. He continued trying to convince everyone to retreat and choose peace, appealing to their better natures and asking for empathy for the local families whose homes they were attacking.

After several minutes, the mob began to calm down, hearing his words, but soon we all noticed the first house on our street at the end of the block had been set on fire by the mob. Within minutes, the wind picked up and the fire spread, quickly engulfing the homes next to it.

The energy in the street shifted as everyone realized the situation had gotten serious and families could die. The will to help in the hearts of some of the mob's members overpowered its collective will to destroy.

The fire department was already busy answering calls all over the city and wouldn't come to help us. If we didn't come together to do something, everything would burn. Our only option was to carry water bucket by bucket down the street from our homes to douse the fire. As we did, a few remaining members of the mob ransacked my family's building. Some of our neighbors, afraid the mob would set our apartment on fire, began trying to help by moving our furniture out onto the footpath. Many of our belongings were broken or misplaced. The money my father had put aside for me for college was lost as well.

Our apartment and everyone we knew survived the violence in the end. As we were all cleaning up, graphic news began to roll in about murders and families being burned alive in their homes. The next day, the government set a strict curfew, and the army drove heavy-duty vehicles through the streets to enforce it. We could only go out for an hour at a time. This went on for two weeks, delaying my trip to Bangalore. I'd be arriving late to college, behind on my studies from day one.

The train ride down to Bangalore was scheduled to take two and a half days, but yet another near-death experience interrupted me. During the journey, the 1984 Sriharikota cyclone, the worst storm to hit the central east coast of India in fifteen years, hit southern India. The train was forced to stop at a rural station in the small city of Nellore and my fellow passengers and I remained stuck inside the train car convinced we'd be derailed as hundred-mile-an-hour winds raged outside. The car swayed and shook violently as the storm destroyed everything around.

Amid the tension, I started talking with some of the other students on their way to college. We were all carrying snacks in our luggage that our families had given us to take to our dorms. Not knowing how long we'd be trapped; we divided our food and water into rations for the seventy-two people in our car to eat and drink. This gesture was repeated by the people in every other car of the train. We waited out the storm together, consuming as little of what we had as we could at a time.

Finally, the wind died down, and we walked outside into the rain. Dead snakes and other animals were strewn across the grass. Everything, as far as the eye could see, had been ravaged. In front of us, a big bridge had collapsed under the weight of falling boulders. Everywhere was flooded, preventing rescue teams from driving through the area, and the wind was still too strong for the army to fly in to evacuate people.

After seven days of waiting, we were finally airlifted to the city of Chennai, known as Madras at the time. From there, I finally made it to my college in Bangalore, nearly a month late.

I showed up at the registrar's office, frazzled and ready to be shown to my dorm. The gentleman working there looked my name up and informed me I no longer had a space at the school but wasn't sure why. After surviving a violent mob, having my college funds lost, and getting caught in a hurricane, I wasn't about to accept that answer. We took the matter to the vice chancellor, who found out someone in the registrar's office had taken a bribe to give my space at the college to someone else. I fought for my right to attend school, and after days of administrative politics, the perpetrator was eventually fired.

Finally, I was permitted to settle into college life, exhausted and away from home for the first time, ready to begin piecing together my future.

"Life is not short, it is finite."

—Dandapani, Hindu monk, author, and
entrepreneur

My college in Bangalore was one of the best agricultural universities in India, but I knew next to nothing about the local area and its politics. Student activism has a rich and ever-evolving history in my home country, with nuances that differ from region to region. People were intensely passionate about topics relating to power, influence, economic dynamics, and the pervasive challenge of corruption. Resistance groups were quick to pop up at any sign of injustice.

During my first week, I encountered an aggressive gang of activists who began knocking at the doors of each lecture hall one day, ordering everyone to come out and join their strike against the school's administration. They wanted to gain control over university funds related to the student union and cafeteria. Everyone around me knew who they were and seemed to be afraid of them. All of them, including my professor, got up and walked out to join the gang, doing what they could to avoid trouble. I stayed seated.

"Why aren't you leaving?" the thugs asked, approaching me. "Get up."

"I came here to attend school. I'm not leaving. I'm staying right here. Your fight is not mine."

They looked at me menacingly, threatening violence, but left to attend the strike. That night, they came to my dorm room with knives and bicycle chains to intimidate me, letting me know they were capable of harm if I chose to defy them again. Still new to college and living on my own, I was scared but also determined to teach them a lesson someday. Amid my anger, however, I heard the voice of the woman I'd spoken with at the Educational Foundation office in New Delhi: "If you want to go abroad, do well at college in India. Then you might be able to go to graduate school on an education visa."

I let my anger against the hoodlums fade and focused instead on the university's beautiful green campus. It was dotted with eucalyptus trees, and the fresh smell of flowers floated through the air. Until then, I hadn't taken school too seriously, but I was on a mission now. I knew I would have to buckle down and commit to everything I wanted to do if I was going to achieve my goals. I started studying hard and getting good grades, which wasn't too hard to do given the culture and environment there.

I also got involved with the university cricket and track teams. I kept a strict schedule every day for four straight years, going to bed at nine and waking up at three in the morning, even when I didn't feel well. My father's early-riser example had created a love inside me of the quiet hours before dawn when I could concentrate on studying while others were asleep. I never missed a single day of class, which was necessary because teachers would surprise us with quizzes we weren't allowed to make up later. In fact, perfect attendance got us five points and was not to be missed, given the competitive nature of the university.

Ravi departing Bangalore after graduation, 1988

My classmates and I became highly disciplined, fighting tooth and nail to compete with one another for the highest scores. At the same time, we also cared deeply for each other, taking notes for anyone who was sick and raising our voices for one another in cases of injustice, like when teachers or campus administration behaved unfairly. This fortified my decision not to feel intimidated by the school's rabid political thugs, but over those four years, I was involved in so many little battles that I knew there was no way I'd be able to stay there for graduate school. One of my professors, for instance, would spend his lectures reading notes to us rather than engaging with the class. I stood up at some point to ask why he became a teacher in the first place.

"Just give us the notes! We'll read them ourselves!"

I was a troublemaker in that way, which lost me points on my GPA, but I never regretted my actions. It was more important to me to follow my heart and speak up for what was right when it felt necessary. I ended up graduating in Agriculture Marketing and Co-operation with honors in 1988. By then, I had written to hundreds of graduate schools worldwide for information about where I could apply and how. After applying to around ten of those schools, I was granted admission to three in the US.

The best offer I received, financially speaking, was from the University of Wisconsin-Platteville. I was ecstatic to receive my letter of acceptance and head back to New Delhi so I could pick up my education visa from the embassy. I would fly there at the end of the year and get a master of sciences in agricultural industries. There was one problem, of course: I was broke.

The night before my trip to the US embassy, I stayed in New Delhi with Sukhvinder Singh, a Sikh friend I'd sat next to in high school. I had spent years getting to know him and his family and was excited to catch up about the four years that had passed while I was at college. The conversation shifted to my plans for the future and the financial worries standing in my way.

"I have no money to buy a plane ticket to America and neither does my family. The exchange rate isn't on my side, either. Ten rupees here in India only comes out to a dollar in America. I don't know how I'll afford it."

Sukhvinder listened intently but had no solution for me. He simply shrugged and said something good might happen, considering how well everything had worked out so far. The next morning, before I headed out as we were having breakfast, his older brother walked into the kitchen and handed me a blank check. I looked at him in bewilderment.

"What's this?"

"It's to pay for your flight. You're going to buy your ticket after you get that visa, Ravi."

"Wh-what?! You—"

"You've done everything in your power to get to this point," he said, "and you're going to that school in the US. Nothing is going to stop you now."

With respect, I tried to decline, knowing the cost of the ticket would likely come out to around $1,000, which felt like a billion at the time. "I don't know when I'll be able to pay you back. It could be years!"

"I'm not asking you to pay me back."

Sukhvinder's family wasn't rich. Not by a long shot. They were middle class at best but had taken me in as one of their own at different points over the years. After much encouragement on Sukhvinder's brother's part, I accepted the check, promising to return the money someday, despite his insistence.

Elated by his kindness, I prepared for my appointment at the American embassy. This was happening.

I arrived at 4:00 a.m. and stood in line with everyone else waiting to speak with the employees at the counter, which opened at 8:00 a.m. You had to get there early, or the line would get too long, and you'd miss your chance to apply that day. There were people there from all backgrounds. Students, businesspeople, researchers, and religious worshippers looking to follow less traditional paths. The crowd teemed with anxious anticipation, wondering whether their visa applications would be approved or denied. Some were already in tears over whatever intense situation they happened to be dealing with. A range of emotions filled the room.

India wasn't as economically versatile in those days. It wasn't the place to start your own business or create a Silicon Valley-esque culture of entrepreneurship. If you wanted to break away from the pressure to become a doctor or lawyer, America seemed like the place to go.

As I waited for my name to be called, I amped myself up with confidence. I had prepared well by speaking with many people who had studied abroad in college, deciding I would simply be myself. When my turn to talk with the mid-thirties American guy at the counter finally came, he asked about my plans for the US.

"You're only twenty-two. What if I grant you a student visa and you never come back?"

I paused to think, then answered his question with another.

"Did you know what you were going to do when you were twenty-two?"

He thought for a moment. "No, I guess not."

"Then isn't that an unfair question to ask?"

"I suppose so."

I went on to tell him I might go to America and love it or hate it but had no idea which was going to happen. My heart pounded as he looked over my papers. Finally, he signaled for me to return to the embassy at 3:00 p.m. that afternoon to collect my visa. I had struck a chord and was given a chance.

Elated, practically walking on air, I called Sukhvinder from a pay phone to tell him the news. Right after, we met and walked to a travel agency together so I could buy my plane ticket.

This was just after Pan Am Flight 103 had exploded over Lockerbie, Scotland, making it the cheapest airline available. They wouldn't take my blank check, however, and we had to call Sukhvinder's brother at work. He rushed over with ₹10,259 rupees (around a thousand US dollars back then) to pay for the ticket.

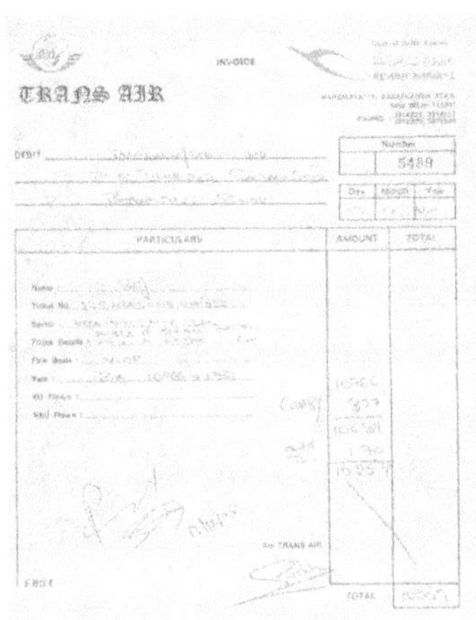

PanAm Airlines receipt, 1988

Ravi and parents on train to New Delhi to catch flight to USA

Ravi with siblings and nephews at home before leaving for New Delhi, December 1988

I felt a huge sense of accomplishment and validation of the hard work I had put in over the past four years. I spent that night with Sukhvinder and his family, then went back to my parents' place to spend a few days there before departing for the US. Still, not everything was in order. I had to find the money I would need in order to survive there, and my dad lost his mind when I brought this up at home.

"Even if you sell my body, we will not have this kind of money, Ravi!"

His anger wasn't truly about the money that day, but the thought of his son leaving to live in a faraway country. My mom, in her diplomatic style, chimed in. "Ravi has worked hard and done everything right in order to get here. He should go, dear."

I know Mom regrets saying that to this day, as I have been living far away from her since. None of us could have foreseen what was in store in the years to come. Dad listened to her in the end, though, and asked all kinds of people for money to help me out. Eventually, a friend of his boss who lived in the US agreed to loan me $2,000, enough (or so I thought) to get by for a while.

On December 28, 1988, I gathered my belongings, said my final good-byes, and headed to the airport with twenty American dollars cash in my pocket and the $2,000 loan I had received in traveler's checks.

As my plane left the runway, I looked out the window and down at my home country; it was shrinking moment by moment before my eyes. I thought back on all I'd done to make it to that point. The whole thing felt a bit crazy, in a way. A single offhand remark from a relative four years earlier had changed the course of my destiny. I wondered what the future held in store. I was leaving everything I'd ever known for a place I'd never been before, and the gap between my expectations and reality would be wide indeed.

University of Life

LESSON #2: AN ELEMENT OF FAITH

I do not recommend a lifestyle based on blind faith or religion. The riches of faith come in the form of belief in ourselves. This asset compounds with time, like money in a bank, provided we remain decisive and take action. Despite life's challenges, you must keep your faith in yourself. What outcomes has faith in yourself created in your life?

THREE

The Big Leap

"The real voyage of discovery consists not in seeking new land-scapes, but in having new eyes."

—Marcel Proust, French novelist and literary critic

ow can you fly on Pan Am after what just happened in the news, Ravi? Just spend a bit more money on a safer airline!

The words of my well-wishers echoed in my mind during the flight from New Delhi to New York, especially when it was announced we'd be diverted to Kuwait without explanation. There had been fear among the general public, including within my family, about Pan Am Airlines after the Flight 103 disaster. In my case, though, I felt completely at ease, riding the high of my excitement and anticipation of what was to come.

A hazy void of uncertainty lay before me. All my assumptions about the United States and what life there would be like were just that: assumptions. My expectations were based on the imagination and optimism of a young, restless heart rather than facts, and not one of them panned out in the way I had envisioned.

From Kuwait, my flight was diverted once more, this time to Geneva for a night, which I assume happened as a result of the barrage of new security measures the airline was rapidly working to put in place. I was unbothered by the delay, excited to be flying and seeing the outside world for the first time. Pan Am put all of us from the flight up in a five-star hotel, all expenses paid. I had never stayed in such a place in all my life. Young and full of boundless energy in those days, I didn't want to sleep and instead stayed up to take it all in. Eating at the table in my room, I stared out the window at the sparkling, snow-covered Swiss Alps, grateful for my warm heater and delicious meal, enjoying the thrill of the moment.

The next morning, they brought us back to the airport, and we boarded our flight from Geneva to New York. Another Indian student sat next to me who had been living in Australia and apparently traveled a lot. As we made conversation, she could tell I was nervous and gave me tips for how to handle life in Western countries. It might be hard to find Indian food and spices, she told me, depending on where I lived. Seeing that I was en route to Wisconsin, that would likely be the case.

I was famished the whole flight, unable to eat the food we were served. I'm vegetarian, and all the meal choices on flights back then contained meat. I had also never eaten anything but Indian food throughout my life. I had no concept of what pasta was. I didn't know what to expect in a Chinese stir-fry. My lack of experience with foreign food made me unable to work up an appetite. Instead, I elected to continue on an empty stomach.

When New York City came into view through the window, my fellow Indian student pointed down at the Statue of Liberty, but I was so hungry that all I could think about was food.

Finally, we landed at JFK airport and disembarked the plane. I sat in the domestic terminal to wait for my American Airlines flight to

Chicago, where I would board a Greyhound bus to Wisconsin. By then, I was weak with hunger, exhausted, and struggling to feel comfortable.

Nearby, there was a vending machine with candy and chips, but I'd never seen one before and didn't quite know what I was looking at. I watched people insert money in exchange for the snacks inside, one after another. I was fascinated and tempted to buy something. I held back though, imagining myself making a mistake and not being able to get my money back.

That twenty dollars in cash was all I had aside from traveler's checks, and losing it would be a huge disappointment.

I saw people drinking from a water fountain, which was also new to me. I didn't know where the water came from or whether it was truly safe to drink. It *seemed* safe, but how could I know for sure? Again, I chose to stay hungry and thirsty.

Suddenly, a man sat next to me. He, I would find out later, was Dr. Mohan Sood, dean of the graduate college at Northeastern Illinois University in Chicago. Though he had an Indian background, he didn't look or sound South Asian. He looked like any typical Caucasian man from the West.

Dr. Sood tried to strike up a conversation with me, asking where I'd come from and where I was going. I was skeptical at first and felt I shouldn't trust him. I'd heard all kinds of stories about different ways global travelers had been taken advantage of by thieves, scammers, and pickpockets. I couldn't afford the possibility of this strange man robbing me. Cautiously, I answered his questions, trying to be evasive and ignore him, hoping he'd leave me alone. All I could focus on was the hunger gnawing at my stomach and my parched throat.

Eventually, Dr. Sood asked whether I had called the friends who were waiting for me in Chicago. Indeed, I had contacts with a group of PhD students, one of whom was the son of a friend of my father's. They had agreed to let me stay with them for a night before I boarded the bus for the final leg of my trip to Wisconsin. I hadn't contacted them, not wanting to spend money on a long-distance call. Dr. Sood had a calling card and offered to help me use it at a pay phone. Hesitant, I accepted and let my friends know over the phone that my original flight had been diverted and I'd be arriving on the next flight. I still didn't know Dr. Sood's name, let alone trust him, but was a bit more open to making conversation with him after that.

We boarded our flight and as it turned out, Dr. Sood was seated next to me on the plane. Again, I couldn't eat any of the meals we were offered. Noticing my distaste for the food, Dr. Sood offered me some crackers from his bag. I took and ate them, unsure why this strange man seemed so intent on helping me.

When we landed in Chicago, Dr. Sood's whole family was there waiting for him, jubilant to see him again. His mother, wife, and two sons hugged him and spoke to him in Hindi. At that moment, I relaxed completely, realizing how paranoid I must have seemed. He was a dedicated family man, not some criminal looking to steal my wallet. He introduced me to each of them and offered to give me a ride to my friends' place, which I gratefully accepted.

As I exited the doctor's car upon arrival at my friends' home, I abruptly learned what "cold" really meant in Chicago.

In India, you'd have to live in the northern mountains to experience such frigid temperatures. I was wholly unprepared in my slacks, shirt, jacket, and brand-new leather dress shoes. Upon taking my very first step, I slipped on the ice and fell flat on the sidewalk. *Bam!* I was lucky not to have broken any bones on my first night in America.

Dr. Sood ran over to help me up and walked me to the door of the house, carrying some of my luggage for me. We exchanged contact information, and I thanked him for his immense kindness, a bit bashful over how things had unfolded during our short time together. He offered to pick me up in the morning and have me over for breakfast before driving me to the bus station. Again, gratefully, I accepted.

My friends invited me into their house, asking how my long trip had been. Luckily, being Indian, they had food there I could eat. I filled my stomach and felt myself coming back to life, then slept like a rock on their spare mattress for the night.

The next morning, Dr. Sood came as promised, had me over for breakfast with him and his family, then dropped me off at the Greyhound station. I waved goodbye and turned to board the bus on my own once more, though far less hungry than before.

I arrived at my final destination in Wisconsin at the stroke of midnight on December 31, 1988, emerging from the bus straight into a wind chill of twenty to thirty degrees below zero. Awaiting me at the station was one of my new professors, Dr. Harold Beals, the man who had written my acceptance letter to the university. He hadn't been responsible for arranging housing for me, however, and asked where I would be staying. I told him I'd been in touch with an Indian graduate student who said I could be his roommate.

Unfortunately, Dr. Beals informed me that the man I'd been contacting had left Wisconsin to attend school in Louisiana and wouldn't be returning.

There I was, halfway around the world, freezing in the middle of the night, at a bus station with my luggage and nowhere to go.

The professor had a plan and brought me to the house of a gentleman named Paras Reddy, an immigrant and businessman from Fiji. He was a tall, strong-looking man with dark reddish eyes, a deep voice, and a mustache. A friend of Dr. Beals, he listened to the story of my situation while sizing me up, visibly emotionless.

"There's a room upstairs," he told me. "You can stay there for seven days. If you don't like it, you can leave."

That was it. With no other option available to me, I quickly agreed.

After helping me take my luggage up to the small bedroom, Dr. Beals said goodbye and Paras went back to bed. There was a kitchenette there, along with a small bathroom and a dinky window by the bed. I sat there and looked out at the snow. Alone, freezing, and hungry once more in an unfamiliar land, I finally cracked. Tears flowed down my face, and I made no attempt to stop them, feeling I'd made the worst decision of my life. The chill of the cold dug down into my bones. None of the clothes I'd brought would be enough to protect me. I stayed awake the entire night thinking of my home in India. The friends and family I'd left behind. The warmth. The food. The familiarity of my culture. It was one of the most desperate moments of my life.

What the hell did I do?

Did I make a mistake?

The next morning at eight, Paras knocked at the door and told me to come downstairs for breakfast. There, he introduced me to his wife, two sons, and daughter. They had prepared orange juice, waffles, and a few other items. I had a little bit of everything to be polite, but still wasn't quite satisfied, which they could clearly see.

After breakfast, Paras told me to get ready, as someone was coming to pick me up. Not knowing who to expect, I did as he told me and heard a knock at the door at 10:30. A short woman with a big smile on her face stood there, beckoning me out to her car where she introduced herself before driving me to her home.

Her name was Dr. Meena Maski, a local pediatrician married to a surgeon. I suspect Professor Beals had informed Dr. Maski I was staying with Paras. He and the international student office had also informed the small community of Indian immigrants in town of my impending arrival.

Within seconds of meeting her, my entire mood was flipped on its head. The way she welcomed me into her house as if I were her own son made me feel right at home, safe in America for the first time.

I learned their family had been living in Platteville for many years. The entire county knew who they were and spoke well of them. They were good to everyone, regardless of origin or background, and a huge source of support for the expat community.

Dr. Maski drove me to a secondhand store to buy boots, thick pants, overcoats, and pots and pans so I could survive there rather than freeze to death during my first week of graduate school. Afterward, she introduced me to some Indian faculty members from the university who were equally kind and welcoming. Over the following two weeks before courses formally started, they'd all pick me up and bring me to their homes for lunch or dinner. Finally, I began to relax, feeling less alone than that first night by the window.

I needed to find a more permanent place to live as soon as possible. Luckily, Paras Reddy was somewhat of an entrepreneur. In addition to working for one of the local banks, he owned a number of properties that he rented out to students. The problem was, I couldn't afford any of them on my own. I'd had a ballpark idea of how far my two thousand dollars would get me in America but had based it on how much I typically had to spend in India. What I hadn't realized was how much each credit hour of my school's curriculum would cost me on top of the stipend for the teaching assistantship I'd been granted by my master's program. The money I'd brought with me wasn't going to cut it. I had to figure out how I was going to sort my finances out, and quickly.

Ravi and his first roommate, Coomar, in America

This was how I met Coomar, a fellow Indian graduate student earning his master's in industrial engineering. Like me, he was on the hunt for a roommate, and someone he knew introduced us. Once he came into the picture, we paid Paras two hundred and fifty dollars for rent and another two fifty for the deposit. That only left me with a bit of money aside from what I needed for tuition and other crucial expenses. I wasn't sure what to think of the arrangement I'd agreed to, but it was the best I could do with what I had.

"Action is the foundational key to all success."

—Pablo Picasso

After securing housing, I dove right into the process of figuring out how I could start working and earning money. At the time, foreign students were allowed to work up to twenty hours a week on campus. I found a job at the library—my first job *ever*—which paid $2.36 an hour. It wasn't much money, particularly by today's standards, but it helped get me by in the short term until I found something better. At the end of the day, though, I was going to need help.

Dr. Maski could see my desperate situation and, out of sheer generosity, offered to loan me money whenever my situation became unbearable. She and her family gave no timeframe for repayment on those loans but trusted I would make good on my word as soon as I could. This not only helped me financially but psychologically as well, motivating me to work hard so I could repay any debts.

During that first week, I was also introduced to Dr. Sukhwal, a professor of geography at the university. He and his wife were incredibly kind, inviting me to their home to talk and share home-cooked meals, helping me relax and begin to feel at home. Had I not gotten their support, along with that of Dr. Sood, Dr. Beals, Paras Reddy, and Dr. Maski, I might have spiraled into depression or ended up in some risky situation. The hospitality of those people provided the safety net I needed to realize that the feelings of loneliness, despair, and hopelessness I had felt my first night were normal for immigrants.

Everyone who helped me had been through the same process in the past. Dr. Sood had come to the States from India in the sixties, he told me, and was initially unable to rent an apartment due to discrimination over his nationality. Dr. Sukhwal and his wife had done hard labor at farms while pursuing their PhDs. Dr. Maski had similar stories of her own to share. I had it relatively easy, all things considered.

Paras, my new landlord, hadn't been particularly "friendly" per se. He was a matter-of-fact guy who never gave me or Coomar an ounce of sympathy, but he had his reasons for his approach. He was an immigrant, too, and had come to the US as a student. He wanted us to understand that nothing came free there. If we were going to make it, we would have to work our butts off just as hard as he did. I was never able to completely relax around him, but that initial fear and hesitation gave way to the insight of what was possible for me.

I learned to embrace uncertainty with patience, always focusing on the next step and what I needed to do to master it. I also quickly realized that I would have to trust the people who offered me help. I wouldn't do so blindly but with the element of faith I had always carried in my heart before that point.

It is only after we've opened up to others that we can learn from their wisdom and build upon it. The harshest transitions of our lives demand that we do. By being open to the help and support of others, I was able to connect with a diverse group of people who became trusted friends and advisors. If I had been closed off and unwilling to trust, I would have missed out on their kindness and generosity. I felt a bit safer and more confident with each week that passed and began to craft a clear vision of my destiny, unaware that life was already preparing to throw yet another curveball my way.

University of Life

LESSON #3: VALUING OUR VILLAGE

There's an African saying that goes, "I am because you are." Our accomplishments, while ours, aren't the result of individual effort. We create them with the influence and help of countless people. Both directly and indirectly, the people in our lives make their impression and keep the wheels of fate turning for us. How has your village helped you move forward?

FOUR

Searching for Solid Ground

"Fall seven times, stand up eight."

—Zen proverb

During the two or so years I spent earning my master's degree in agricultural industries at the University of Wisconsin-Platteville, I slowly but surely got the hang of life in America. Upon arrival, I noticed the houses were all built differently, made from wood or stone rather than concrete, like they were in India. People always kept their windows closed to keep the heat in, which was an issue for me when others would cook food that didn't suit my tastes in the kitchen. I would open my windows at times to air the smell out of my room, accustomed to fresh air.

The landscape was different as well. While India is known for its beautiful jungles and mountains, I'd never seen rolling fields like those that characterized the Wisconsin countryside or the barns where people kept their cows. And the weather, falling below zero in the winter by twenty degrees Fahrenheit or more, was so shockingly cold that I couldn't believe businesses were able to run reliably. People worked and went to class no matter how cold it got. Just walking outside could freeze your skin, a prickly, numbing sensation I'd never experienced in India. Ice would collect in the corners of our eyes, and the threat of hypothermia was always present.

I was also struck by the differing habits of the locals. People were open, outgoing, and very into partying, which I had never experienced in my home country. We would hang out and play cricket in India, but never went to clubs or threw house parties with kegs. At the same time, people demonstrated an impressively strong work ethic. Almost every local undergrad at school had work experience already, usually related to farming or fixing things, and I admired their skills. They also dressed more formally, wearing professional suits to college seminars, emphasizing the importance of appearance in America. I felt judged at times for showing up to events in slacks and a jacket that didn't quite match, but they were all I could afford.

People's eating habits surprised me as well. They would drink milk by the gallon right out of the bottle, eat bloody slabs of steak, and consume what felt like an unreasonable amount of cream cheese on a regular basis. Bagels, burgers, brownies, and microwaveable TV dinners were the norm. I once watched a giant apple pie get eaten in its entirety by two people. Portions were huge, and the meals themselves felt too heavy, as someone who had been raised on fresh, plant-based foods my whole life.

Car culture in America was different as well. We only had two or three brands available in India at the time and the roads we drove on were cracked, full of rocks and potholes, or unpaved entirely. Abundance, sleekness, and variety reigned supreme in Wisconsin. People loved their cars and relished driving them fast down smooth, flat highways stretching as far as the eye could see, past Kmart, Walmart, and other grand, mart-esque empires packed with overwhelming amounts of goods.

While the local culture of Platteville, rural and quaint, offered an endless stream of small surprises, most of my first two years in the States were spent on campus. There was always some kind of challenge lurking around the corner at school, waiting to surprise me along the way. I had never touched a computer, for instance, and didn't know how to type or use the software needed to write my term papers. Learning these skills took a tremendous amount of hand-holding from Coomar during my first semester. I was also shocked when my first term paper was returned to me covered in red marks correcting my spelling mistakes, given that I'd learned to write in British English rather than American English in India.

These small challenges added up over time. It was frustrating to have to constantly rewire my brain in order to get by, but none of this held a candle to my main concern: money.

To say my finances were tight would be an understatement. Between working at the library and fulfilling my job as a teaching assistant, I was barely scraping by with $1,863 per semester. I'd end up leaving the graduate student office at two or three in the morning each day to catch a few hours of sleep back at home, then be up before dawn to prepare for the day's classes.

Coomar and I shopped for groceries twice a month and rationed out our food at home. Aware of our money troubles, families of Indian origin in Platteville would frequently invite us over for lunch or dinner and would invariably pack food for us to take when we left. The town didn't have a huge Indian expat community—maybe twenty families, at most—but people were eager to meet and support one another, as if it were their duty to care for newbies to America like myself. This played a pivotal role in our survival. On countless occasions, we'd get home late at night to find frozen food waiting on our doorstep, which was always a godsend. To this day, I'm still grateful for the endless love and kindness of those people.

In spite of all the help we received, I went hungry on a regular basis. I would cope by drinking water or going for a run to take my mind off the pain gripping my body. On campus, I would walk into the cafeterias looking for leftover food, eating scraps off abandoned plates while no one was watching. When people invited me to parties, I would make excuses not to go, telling them I had to study. I couldn't afford to contribute or buy anyone gifts as a thank-you gesture. My only priorities were studying and making ends meet; I had to avoid any and all unnecessary expenses, even if it meant missing out on having a typical college social life.

Coomar had a former host mom from a family in town, Mrs. Jones. Every time I went to her home with him, the energy was inviting. Her three little boys were fond of me and the Indian chai tea I would make for them. One day, which I'll never forget, she invited me to see a movie with their family. I eagerly accepted, looking forward to an outing in Dubuque, Iowa, just a short drive from Platteville. It was my first time to see a movie in a theater since I arrived in the US.

When we got to the front of the line, Mrs. Jones bought tickets for her and her kids, then signaled for me to buy my own. I froze, knowing I only had two dollars in my pocket. Luckily, that was the price of the ticket. I was able to pay but learned a huge cultural lesson.

In India, when we invite someone out somewhere, we always pay for them, and I expected the same in the States. As it turned out, the practice was far rarer, and after that, I never accepted any invitation that remotely involved money.

In spite of it all, I was doing well in school and building good relationships with the people around me. I loved Platteville and still consider it my second home to this day. Every day brought new experiences I could learn from, and people there were kind and honest, often leaving their front doors unlocked. But those two years were also filled with loneliness. There were no cell phones or online platforms for making international calls back then, which were so expensive that when I did call my family in India, our conversations could only last about thirty seconds.

"How are you guys doing? Okay, good. Yeah, I'm fine. Hey, gotta go! Love you!"

I wrote long letters to my family, and they returned the favor, but the wait for a response could take anywhere from two to six weeks. It's hard to describe the feeling of anticipation I had while waiting for those letters. Part of me still misses it. Emails and DMs are too impersonal for me these days. There's something special about holding a letter from someone you miss in your hands, knowing it had been held by them too.

Winter in Wisconsin is not for the faint of heart. At that time, Coomar and I were two of only a handful of students who didn't have a car. People would drive by as we walked to and from class on campus, knee-deep in freezing snow. Sometimes the local police would take pity on us and stop to give us a ride. For the most part, though, we got around on foot and had to depend on others to take us long distances or act as chauffeur while we went shopping. As the weather got colder, we knew there was no way we could go on battling the elements. We needed a car.

I told everyone I knew that I was in the market for a vehicle without any plan in my mind for how I'd find the money to pay for it. Out of the blue one day, Paras called Coomar and me and told us to meet him at the bank where he worked. Apparently, he had a car there that we'd be able to afford (although the price I could truly afford was south of zero at the time).

Intrigued, Coomar and I made our way to the bank, and Paras met us in the parking lot, carrying a key. We looked around at the mounds of snow surrounding us; there wasn't a single car in sight. Paras pointed, directing our attention to a shiny bit of blue peeking out from the blanket of white. Coomar and I looked at each other, thinking this must be some kind of joke, while our landlord fetched a shovel from inside the bank.

1977 Malibu Classic example
(without the rust from Ravi's car)

Once Paras had cleared the snow, Coomar and I could see the entirety of the rusted 1977 Chevrolet Malibu Classic we'd gone there to check out.

"It's a piece of junk, Paras!" Coomar said. "I bet it won't even start."

To our surprise, Paras unlocked the door and started the engine with no issues. It rumbled to life as we looked on, impressed he even managed to get the door open in one piece with how rusted it was.

"The owner is selling this car as-is for 350 dollars."

Now that may not sound like much today, but it felt like a *fortune* back then, especially for a couple of broke college immigrants like us. Disappointed over the condition of the car, Coomar and I hesitated, eyeing each other skeptically.

"Remember," Paras said, reading our minds, "you have no money. This might be the best you can do for now."

That sprinkling of reality shook us out of our high expectations. He was right. Our chances of finding something in better shape were slim to none.

"Look," he continued, "this car is perfect for driving around town. If you stay local, you'll be fine. But you're going to need to replace the battery and all four tires as well."

Hah!—so we'd need *more* than $350 to get the car in working condition. He could've mentioned that beforehand! Regardless, we at least had an option to consider and left the bank in search of a way to buy our new-old Chevy.

A few days later, I ran into a friend from Pakistan on campus. Like me, he was an immigrant on a student visa and told me our school offered loans of up to $350 dollars to international students for emergencies. If I could get that money and manage to pay it back, I could actually begin building a proper credit history in America, which I knew I would need. But was my situation really an *emergency*?

Hell yes it was!

I was walking in the snow every day to get to and from class. If I caught the flu in this weather, it could kill me!

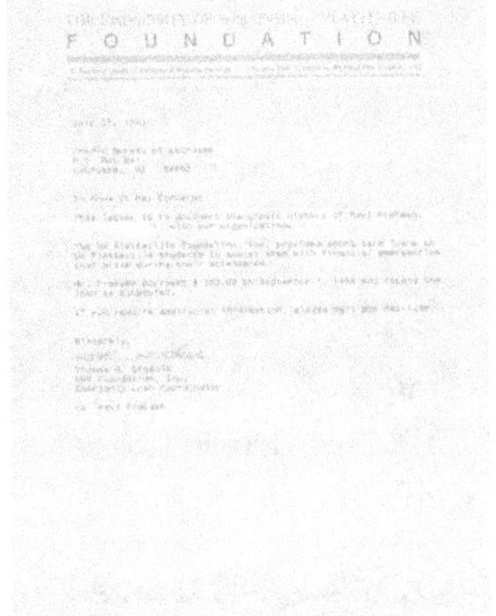

Receipt from the University of Wisconsin Foundation

Thankfully, the staff at school were empathetic to our plight. I was granted the loan and immediately bought the car.

Soon after the sale, Dr. Beals, ever my mentor and savior in desperate times, spoke with someone at a local garage who agreed to replace the car's battery and all four tires for 150 dollars. Coomar agreed to loan me the cash to cover it. I had the car dropped off at the garage, and the wonderful guys who worked there assured me they'd take care of everything.

"Come back in four or five hours. We'll have it ready for you to drive."

We went on our way, heading home to take a nap, but by the time we got there, we couldn't find the money Coomar had withdrawn from the bank. We must have dropped it somewhere but had no idea where. In a panic, we looked at each other, wondering what we would do. A hundred and fifty dollars was a fortune for us at that point. We backtracked, retraced our steps, and talked to anyone in downtown Platteville who would listen to us, asking if they'd happened to see 150 dollars in cash lying around, to no avail. Defeated, we made our way back to the garage.

Once again, the unseen forces of the universe came to our rescue. The guys at the car shop were kind enough to let us pay them back in installments. I was so relieved, I literally cried in that moment, happy to find a way out of our crisis.

Afterward, Coomar and I filed a police report, knowing our odds of getting that missing money back were slim. A couple months later, however, the cops called us and let us know it had been found and returned by some honest citizen. We'd dropped the whole wad of money outside near the bank. After we picked it up from the police station, we were able to pay our friends at the garage immediately, eternally grateful for their trust in us.

Once the car finally worked and was ready to drive, our next challenge was getting a driver's license.

Neither of us had ever driven a car before coming to America, and we had no money to pay for lessons. So, naturally, we decided to teach ourselves how to drive. What could possibly go wrong?

Behind the house we rented from Paras, there was a dirt road and a small green area. While reading a book about how to pass the driving test, we drove the car up and down that road and over the lawn. Eventually, we felt ready to take it for a spin around town away from the prying eyes of our neighbors, who certainly didn't appreciate our clever initiative. As it turned out, Paras didn't appreciate it either. When he came to collect the following month's rent and saw how much we'd torn up the backyard, he lost it.

"What the hell were you two thinking?! Go to driving school and practice there!"

It was my turn to politely remind him what he'd told us when we first saw the car.

"Remember, Paras, we have no money. This is the best we can do for now."

He left in a huff that day, grumbling to himself, but we could tell he understood.

Coomar took the driving test first and failed. Turns out parallel parking a huge Malibu Classic isn't so easy for a novice. I went to work on perfecting my parallel parking skills and was able to pass the test on the first try. After a bit more practice, Coomar finally passed as well, and we were ready to hit the road together.

News that we'd gotten a car spread fast among the international student community on campus. I soon found myself driving everyone and their mother to grocery stores, department stores, and job interviews. I didn't feel like I could turn down any of their requests after all the walking Coomar and I had done in the freezing cold. I was happy to help, but struggled to pay for gas, even at $0.85 a gallon.

After gaining more faith in our driving abilities, Coomar and I started taking the car on longer drives, visiting Chicago to eat at Indian restaurants with our friends. It was 180 miles each way, but the distance was worth the satisfaction we got from our newfound freedom.

The summer of 1989 finally approached, which meant Coomar would graduate soon. He was looking for a job and had gotten a call to interview at a precision engineering company in Rockford, Illinois. Though the place was 100 miles away, I drove him to the interview in the sweltering heat. I was content to do it, but eventually realized that while I was helping others in need, I wasn't doing much in the way of helping myself and still didn't know what I'd do after graduation.

Coomar ended up leaving Platteville in August to pursue his second master's degree in engineering at the University of Wisconsin in Milwaukee. His absence left a gaping void in my life. He was my first roommate and friend in the US. We would have long conversations about how we might make it in the world one day and what that might look and feel like. We would observe the stark differences between

India and the USA—the people, the commotion, the talks, the food, the music, and the traffic. I missed those moments we spent together, but being on my own did end up boosting my sense of independence.

Determined to expand my horizons and better understand the world, I decided to look for a new place with housemates from cultures different from my own. I soon found a room in a place that was 150 years old and housed four other international students. It had old hardwood floors that groaned and creaked with each step, evoking a sense of the past. My new housemates included Jackson from Liberia, a fellow grad student in the Agricultural Industries department; Khan, an undergraduate student from Pakistan whose parents were based in the United Arab Emirates; and Richard, another undergraduate student from Nigeria studying engineering. We all got along well and worked hard at our studies, but the overall experience of living there was one I couldn't make sense of.

All around us in our neighborhood, we were exposed to twenty-four hours of out-in-the-open drinking and debauchery from students living in the sorority and frat houses. This was the case from the very first week of the school year and even went on during exam weeks. How did they have so much free time to party while students like us were struggling to find time to sleep, given our workload between school and work? We would talk about this as we ate around the dining table, shocked at how normal the party scene was to Americans. Drinking wasn't looked upon favorably in our countries, and we had come to the US to make progress in life, not get wasted.

<hr>

Thinking hard about my future, I focused on what my next steps would be after completing my master's program.

<hr>

Having been exposed to many inspiring professors at the University of Wisconsin, my subconscious began percolating with dreams of earning a PhD in economics. I had spent two full hours there with agronomist

Norman Ernest Borlaug, winner of the Nobel Prize for Life Sciences, known the world over for his "Green Revolution."

I had also been gaining interest in the concept of the European Union, which ended up being finalized four years later in 1993. During my research on the subject, I learned about a man named Dr. Phillip Abbot, an authority in the field at Purdue University in Indiana. He shared my interest in the economic impact of the formation of the European Union and the prospect of studying under his lead lit me up with excitement.

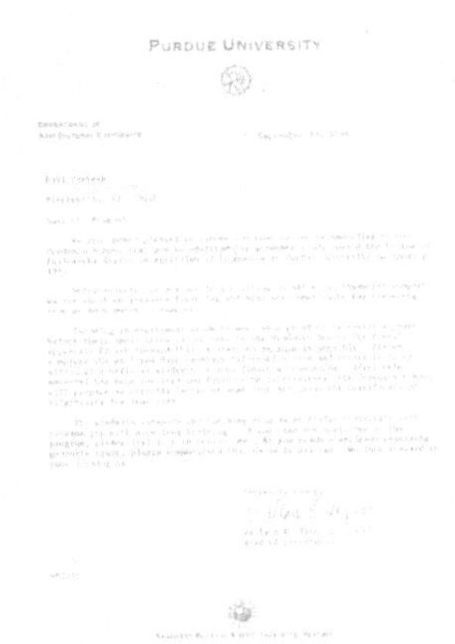

Acceptance letter from Purdue University

I was so confident about my chances of getting into Purdue that it was the only PhD program I applied to. I was indeed accepted, much to my relief, which took the huge weight of the question of my next steps off my shoulders.

When fall arrived, I drove to Purdue to see Dr. Abbot in person. It was incredible not only to meet him but also to visit the campus and visualize myself studying there someday. Dr. Abbot informed me I would need to come up with five or six thousand dollars for my first semester. He was impressed by my life story and promised that if I did well in my courses, he would arrange my funds for the remainder of the program. Additionally, because I was an international student, I would need to show I had access to $20,000 for the school year to get my I-20 form, which was necessary for the student visa I needed to remain in the US legally. In my mind, this was all achievable. I thanked Dr. Abbot for his advice and returned to Platteville in a whirlwind of excitement, picturing myself taking notes in the lecture halls of Purdue.

Christmas break rolled around that year, and my housemates all returned home to their families, leaving me alone in our huge, old house, dangerously broke. Struggling with hunger, I hoped someone might extend an invitation to spend Christmas with them, but no such thing materialized.

With the few pennies I had to my name, I gathered the courage to approach the manager of Dick's, a local grocery store, and showed him my meager coins. Moved by my desperation, he gave me a loaf of bread and some apples that would otherwise have been thrown out. I froze in that house, pained by hunger, huddled on my mattress, which lay on my floor without a frame. I rationed the food I was given and ate it slowly, often subsisting solely on water and small bites of bread.

Through determination, I managed to get through that period, enduring until my housemates came home in January. They brought food with them, thankfully, marking the end of my solitary struggle for sustenance.

I was ninety percent of the way through my master's program in Platteville by then and was offered the option to extend the deadline for turning in my thesis, free of charge. This worked out in my favor, given I would then have eight to ten months to save the $6,000 I needed to start my PhD program at Purdue in the fall of 1990.

Ecstatic about my plan, I called Coomar in Milwaukee to share the news. He told me he'd do whatever he could to help me make it happen and invited me to stay at his place so I could sleep on his spare mattress while looking for a job. I took him up on his offer, knowing my prospects would be better in a big city that wasn't overrun by college students. Soon enough, I got a part-time work permit from my university and landed a job as a night-shift cashier at a Milwaukee convenience store.

Upon starting the job, I realized I would be working alone all night in a risky, run-down neighborhood. My list of duties included tidying up the store, scrubbing the toilets, mopping, stocking shelves, making coffee, cooking hot dogs, sweeping the parking lot, serving donuts, and working the register. The store was surprisingly busy throughout the night. People would come in at all hours to buy food, coffee, booze, and lottery tickets. Some of the regulars were aggressive, always hungover, drunk, or in the process of getting there. Others would come in and spend $200 on lottery tickets daily. There I was making minimum wage, $2.36 an hour, and the people I was serving were throwing away their money.

From January 1990, I spent the remainder of my graduate program working at the store while putting together my thesis. Several times a month, I would drive the 150 miles to Platteville after my night shift to meet with my graduate advisor, Dr. Cropp. I would then drive back to Milwaukee with just enough time to eat, rest my eyes, and return to work at seven p.m.

My priorities were to support myself, pay back Dr. Maski, who I owed around ten thousand bucks, and save money for my PhD program at Purdue. Food was merely an afterthought. I mostly survived on water, fruit, vegetables, and, of course, ramen noodles. Two or three weeks into my new lifestyle, working all night began taking its toll on my body. I had no time to work out and never slept more than a few hours at a time.

I was exhausted, but kept going in spite of it all, singularly focused. The thought of becoming an illegal immigrant or being forced to return to India (before I'd gotten my PhD, at least) was unbearable. Failure was not an option.

After a couple months of working in Milwaukee, someone introduced me to a professor from the university there. The man listened to my story and offered me a job working for him on an environmental project in Michigan from May to August of that year. The opportunity would guarantee I'd be able to save the $6,000 I needed for Purdue *and* be able to pay off my debt to Dr. Maski quickly. I couldn't have been more grateful for my luck in that moment, thanking the universe for another benevolent surprise. I left my meeting with him cautiously optimistic that all my financial woes would work out after all.

At the university in Platteville, Coomar and I had known a highly respected professor of computer science who was an expert in his field. He and his wife had always been kind to us, inviting us and our friends over for lunch or dinner. They had treated me like family and were well aware of how the I-20 process worked. The professor agreed to act as my sponsor, take care of my PhD application paperwork, and let Purdue know I would have the $20,000 in necessary funds.

I was over the moon. Finally, the last piece of the puzzle had come into place. All I had to do now was concentrate on finishing my thesis and work hard to save the money I needed for the fall. I assured him and his wife I would not need a penny from them, confident that I would have the money to support myself by August.

One April night at the convenience store, I was mopping the floor when two guys barged in to steal beer. They had a gun but didn't use it, and I went home thankful to be alive after they left. The next morning, I went to the police station to file a report and identify the culprits. The cops showed me photos of the criminals they had on file. To my shock, several of my regular customers at the store were on their local wanted list. The cops wouldn't give me the details of their crimes but told me the file they'd opened was for people who had done something serious.

> Exhausted and shaken up, I made my way to Coomar's apartment afterward. I was hungry but couldn't eat. My gut was telling me I needed to get out of that job fast.

The comments from the cops were spinning in my head, filling my imagination with visions of what might happen to me if I stayed.

Within three weeks, I'd be on my way to Michigan for my job with the environmental project, but it might be too late by then. I was afraid for my life.

On a whim, I decided to change course and stop by the house of the University of Wisconsin-Milwaukee professor I'd be working with to see if I could start early and quit my current job. When I arrived at his house, the professor was surprised to see me. I asked about the job, and, to my complete devastation, he told me it was no longer available. He had offered it to his brother-in-law instead, unbeknownst to me.

I was furious. "When exactly were you going to tell me you'd gone back on your word, if I hadn't shown up unannounced at your doorstep?"

The man was shameless. "Look, it didn't work out. There's nothing I can do for you at this point."

Locking eyes with him, I firmly told him I would make something happen for myself. I also told him never to give anyone false hope ever again, as their life may depend on it. It's better to say no upfront than string someone along out of cowardice. With that, I turned and left.

Armed with my latest news, I raced to Coomar's apartment, determined to find another way to make money over the summer. The next day, I called Purdue to ask about the status of my I-20 form. I was told they had sent the paperwork to the professor in Platteville who had promised to sponsor me and were awaiting his response.

The next morning at 7:30 a.m. when I got off work at the convenience store, I drove to Platteville to meet with the professor and ask for an update. After arriving at his house and sharing a meal with him, he informed me that he couldn't sign the papers like he'd promised. His wife had objected to him acting as my sponsor, fearing he'd be held liable for $20,000 on my behalf. He was ashamed of letting me down but sincere in his words.

Right there and then, I broke down in tears, begging him to give me a chance. I told him I was working night and day to save enough money, so he'd never have to give me a penny. I reminded him of all the people I'd borrowed money from and paid back over the past year while making $2.36 an hour. My pleas were not enough in the end. He apologized for the situation, and I left his home in pieces.

Letter from Dr. Abbott acknowledging Ravi's note as to why he could make it to Purdue

My entire plan for my future had fallen apart in a matter of days. I had worked so hard to put all my eggs in a basket that no longer existed. Over the next few days, I drove around Platteville, knocking on the doors of anyone who had ever said hello or locked eyes with me to ask if they could be my sponsor, but to no avail. There and then, my dream of earning an economics PhD at Purdue came to an end.

I nearly threw up while driving back to Milwaukee. I had no other options. No other sponsors. No other offers from schools aside from Purdue. If I didn't make it into another school by that fall, I would become an illegal alien in America.

I needed to come up with a new plan fast, so I reached out to my mentor in Platteville, Dr. Harold Beals, telling him I wanted to earn a second master's degree, this time in agricultural economics with an emphasis on international trade. I asked for his help with recommendation letters, applications, and phone calls to schools that might be willing to accept me at the last minute.

We had no internet yet in 1990 to use for research. Application fees were steep, and long-distance phone calls were expensive, but I had done well at Platteville and had a good reputation. After speaking with Dr. Beals, all my professors came through for me and did everything in their power to help.

I drove back to Milwaukee to quit my job at the convenience store, certain I wouldn't last another night. As it later turned out, the student who got hired to replace me was shot dead during an armed robbery on his first shift. I was horrified by the news and counted my blessings, thankful my time on this planet wasn't up yet.

The universe had more chances in store for me. In an odd way, I felt like a cat with nine lives.

Back in Platteville once more, I found a cheap room to rent in a house with three students from Spain. Shortly after signing the lease, they went back to Europe for the summer, leaving me alone there. I struggled to find work, unable to even get a job washing dishes. That luckily changed when I ran into one of my previous roommates, a local who was born and raised there in Wisconsin. He asked how things were going, and I told him about my unemployment issues.

"What questions did the managers ask you when you went to apply at those places?" he asked.

"Most just wanted to know how long I'd be available to work there," I told him. "If all goes well, I'll only be there through the summer. I need to leave in fall to get my next master's degree somewhere. This is just temporary."

His eyebrows rose in surprise. "You haven't actually been telling them that though, right?"

"Well, yes. I've been honest, of course."

He scoffed and told me to lie. "No one will hire you for three months, Ravi. Tell them you'll be available to work the whole school year!"

I felt uncomfortable following his advice but knew he was right. First and foremost, I put all my focus on applying to grad schools to earn another master's, this time in agricultural economics. Dr. Beals helped me send out paperwork to ten schools and covered the application fees as well. Some schools even agreed to waive the fees altogether, which went a long way in helping me breathe. As I waited for their responses, I went back out to apply for jobs at local businesses, this time telling them I'd be available to work the whole school year.

I immediately got three offers and accepted them all.

Two of my new jobs were in Dodgeville, located about thirty miles from Platteville. I would wake up at 3:30 a.m., shower, eat breakfast, and get to work to start my 5:00 a.m. shift at the Land's End clothing catalog company as a packer. The job involved standing the whole time, moving only my upper body. Clothes that customers had ordered would drop down from a conveyor belt. I had to match the order with its order slip, put both in a box, and drop it back onto the conveyor belt. There were strict quotas for how many boxes we needed to pack per hour, meaning there was no time to rest or make chit chat.

My shift at the catalog company would end at 11:00 a.m. Exhausted, I would drive over to the local Hardee's to start my second job working the register there at noon. Though I had only been hired as a cashier, it turned out everyone at the restaurant was responsible for preparing the food, mopping the floor, and scrubbing the toilets too.

After finishing my Hardee's shift at 6:00 p.m., I would then drive the thirty miles back to Platteville to work as a chef at Pizza Hut from seven to midnight or later, depending on how business went that night. Then I would finally go home, sleep for an hour or two, get up at 3:30, and start the process again. I did this every day throughout the entire summer seven days a week. I was absolutely desperate and felt I had no other choice but to prove to myself I could accomplish what I had set out to do.

By July, I managed to pay off all my debts to people in Platteville. I had to keep my word and get it done so I could focus on making money for the fall semester, wherever I ended up. Many days, I would doze off while driving between jobs and find myself on the wrong side of the road. I'm not proud of that. It was a very hard time. I'd come home stinking of pizza in the middle of the night, disgusted by the smell, and have to scrub my skin to get it off. But before that, I'd check my answering machine to see if I had any messages from any of the graduate schools I'd applied to. Day after day after day, nothing. No response. The anxiety in the pit of my stomach grew and grew.

> *"We do not fear the unknown. We fear what we project onto the unknown."*
>
> —Teal Swan, American speaker and author

Acceptance and offer letter from the University of Idaho

In the second week of July, all my persistence paid off. I came home to messages of acceptance from three universities, which included an offer from Moscow, Idaho, and it was the best choice, financially speaking. There I was about to end my rental agreement in the second week of August, finally getting the break I needed to stay in America legally. I had to report to my school in Idaho by August 20, giving me around three weeks to tie up loose ends in Platteville, move, and make my transition to my new school.

I remember the distinct feeling that I was finally growing from a boy into a man. I was making life-changing decisions with little guidance, flexible enough to pivot in the name of progress rather than getting paralyzed by life's ups and downs. Yet, I missed my family and friends both for support and to share the joy. With each curveball thrown my way, I dug in deep and asked myself what other options I had, what more I could do, who I could ask, who I could connect with, who I could help, and so on. I had fallen so many times but got back up each and every time to try again, just as I had at my father's direction when I took another ride around our ring road on his scooter in Sindri as a boy. After enough practice at this, part of me began to feel unstoppable yet vulnerable enough to know I would need others to move forward.

I left Wisconsin in my now-infamous 1977 Malibu Classic with no working A/C or radio on August 2, 1990, the day Iraq invaded Kuwait, marking the beginning of the Gulf War. Once again, the local mechanic had been kind enough to help me out free of charge, giving the car a tune-up to ensure it would make it to Idaho. I had an exceptionally emotional send-off from my university's faculty members and everyone else who had become my family in Platteville who had helped me settle into life in a foreign land.

Camera and ice box, gift from the Maskis

Dr. Maski and his wife gave me some money for the journey. They also gave me a camera as a graduation gift and an icebox filled with food. I still have both (minus the food) as tokens of respect for them and symbols of my strength.

I left town with a sense of youthful exuberance and freedom, open to all of life's possibilities. As I drove, I left the stressful memories of each curveball I'd overcome behind me. My stress level ticked back up again, however, when the price of gas jumped from $0.85 cents a gallon to $1.05 as I crossed into Iowa.

Life is not for the faint of heart. I knew growing up in India had prepared me to handle adversity, but I would never let those circumstances, or any others, define me. I kept my element of faith, assured that the invisible hands guiding me would always come to my rescue, provided I was taking action.

University of Life

LESSON #4: INNER LEADERSHIP

Leadership, as they say, is an inside job. We must learn to lead and guide ourselves before we can do the same for others. Cultivating curiosity about people, places, and things advances our journey of self-discovery. In what ways do you lead and guide yourself?

FIVE

A New Start in Idaho

*"Between stimulus and response there is a space. In that space
is our power to choose our response. In our response lies
our growth and our freedom."*

—Viktor E. Frankl, Austrian psychiatrist, author, and
Holocaust survivor

I've always been inspired by uncertainty. It was clear that no matter what lay ahead of me in Idaho, I would have to make the most of the opportunity that awaited me there. To dream of success wasn't enough. I would have to stay in action. I'd have to continually rewire myself to adjust to life's circumstances if I was going to maintain any level of stability in the US.

I had loved Wisconsin but was eager to leave behind my memories of the freezing weather, nonstop work and study, constant financial stress, lack of food, exhaustion, danger, and the entire Purdue crisis I experienced there. During the drive to Idaho, I let myself relax and decompress from the struggle, taking a full week to make the trip, stopping to view the countryside along the way. While buying gas, I would ask people what there was to see in the area. On the recommendation of a few people, I visited the Mitchell Corn Palace, a beautiful building in South Dakota with breathtaking indoor murals painstakingly made of thousands of colorful kernels. I also stopped by Badlands National Park, a dry, vast area of geological formations known for its ancient dinosaur fossils. Paying to sleep at hotels along the way was out of the question, of course. Instead, I would pull over and sleep in my car on the side of the highway. Sometimes state troopers would wake me up to check on me. The endless sky, wide-open land, and stunning views were exactly what I needed. I felt at one with the environment, lost in the natural beauty surrounding me, certain that one day, my day would come. I'd find my way somehow.

Ravi in the Badlands

Ravi at a rest area with his rusty 1977 Malibu Classic

Along the border of Wyoming and Montana, I spotted a man on the side of the road trying to hitch a ride. For a moment, I wondered whether I should keep driving, having read about violent crime around the country, but something in my heart told me to stop. A ways down the road, I pulled over, and he ran after me to catch up. My cricket bat was next to me by the driver's side door, just in case he tried any funny business.

I never got my passenger's name, but he was Native American. Though I had read a bit about the region's indigenous tribes, I had never met anyone like him in person. I was so naive about US history that I wondered if these American "Indians" were somehow related to people like me from the Indian subcontinent. (I suppose I wasn't the only one— even Christopher Columbus mistook them as Indian!)

We had a wonderful couple of hours talking as I drove. He told me about his tribe and what life was like for them on the reservation. It made me sad to hear about the suffering and mistreatment Native Americans endured when the Europeans came to this continent. I started wishing we could have more time together, as it was the first time I'd had someone to talk with since leaving Wisconsin. I ended up dropping him off in Billings, Montana, with a bear hug, which I gave him as a sign of friendship, understanding, and thanks for letting me be on his land.

After a week or so of driving, I finally arrived at the campus of the University of Idaho in the small city of Moscow. I went straight to the international student office, and the staff there was outstanding in setting me up for my master's program in agricultural economics. They had everything in place for me to get started on the right foot, including the name of another graduate student, Bill, who was also looking for a roommate. I then walked to the Department of Biochemistry building where he was a doctoral student. Bill was a calm, laid-back guy from Chicago, and as luck would have it, we hit it off right away. That evening, I walked with him to my new apartment to sign the rental contract, which is where I ended up living for my entire two years in the state.

Unlike in Wisconsin, I had a roof over my head from day one in Idaho. A definite sign of progress!

Classes started a few days after I arrived. I shared a graduate student office with three other students—two from China and one from Utah. There were other graduate student offices in the building, and everyone got along well. Our program had people from Pakistan, China, Nepal, Thailand, India, and various states across the US.

I'd been offered in-state tuition and a research assistantship of about $620 per month. All my years of managing my budget down to the penny came in handy again. If I was lucky, I'd be able to pay my $125 rent, $50 for utilities, $50 for phone calls, $100 for food, my fees for school, and still have a bit of money left over. Funds were tight as usual, and I was continually struggling to make ends meet. I maintained a spreadsheet to keep track of the debts I'd accumulated, always making the minimum payment to stay on top of things.

Ravi playing cricket in Idaho

Early on in my studies, I secured a seat in the Graduate Student Union and fought for various issues that we grad students considered important. Being a former devoted cricket player, I petitioned the administration for funding to form a cricket team on campus. As it turned out, students from cricket-playing countries had been attending the university since 1910. After much deliberation, I was able to secure funding that allowed me and my fellow graduate students to form a joint cricket club with the University of Washington-Pullman, located seven miles away. We sent students to various cricket playing countries to buy equipment for the team and convinced our university to build a real cricket pitch.

We were hardcore cricket lovers who played rain or shine. We played our first match against Boeing-Seattle, which ended up being a huge hit with our small college town. Several local businesses had sponsored the event, the largest of which was Pizza Hut (my former employer). They donated so much pizza that all 400 spectators were able to get a slice or two alongside the players. I formed lifelong friendships, thanks to that club, that were never transactional, which I'm grateful for to this day.

*"Wear gratitude like a cloak and it will feed every corner of
your life. If you are irritated by every rub, how will you be
polished?"*

—Rumi, poet, theologian, and scholar

My assistantship didn't provide funding during the summer, so by May 1991, I was desperately brainstorming how I could make additional income over the following few months. At one point, I met a guy on campus who told me he worked on fishing boats for half the year. He assured me I could make good money that way if I was willing to work in Alaska over the summer. I got in touch with some of the companies he referred me to, which promptly sent me recruitment brochures in the mail. I was thrilled to know it was a viable option, even for immigrants, until a friend sat me down and told me about the reality of a job like that.

"Ravi, would you be okay being splashed by freezing waters and seeing blood everywhere? You want to cut fish all day and have that smell on you all the time? Really, Ravi?"

As a vegetarian, I couldn't handle the thought. I nearly threw up imagining the picture he painted for me, and my interest in a career on the high seas was brought to an abrupt end.

Soon after, someone else told me about an on-campus job fixing dorm rooms and working in the cafeteria.

Another graduate student from India, who was eavesdropping on our conversation and also short on money, scoffed at my interest in the position. "How could you think of doing a job like that, coming from a nice Indian family like yours? What would people say?"

I didn't respond to his judgments. I had scrubbed toilets at past jobs and was willing to do whatever it took to make my way in the world. I applied to the job on campus, was promptly hired, and worked hard all summer without a care what anyone thought of it.

As luck would have it, however, one of my professors received some unexpected grant money for a research project a few weeks later and offered it to me for the remainder of the summer, which helped put me at ease. Once again, the universe was looking out for me.

One June morning in 1991, I was riding my bike to school when a brand-new Mercedes Benz took a sharp right turn without warning, pulling right in front of me. I had to react fast to avoid being mowed down and ended up colliding with the front passenger door instead. The impact left a hole in the body of the car.

I jumped off my bike and was on my feet quickly. Other students on their way to school had seen what happened and rushed over to help. Eventually the driver of the car, a middle-aged Caucasian man, walked over and asked whether I was okay. I told him I thought I was fine and needed to leave immediately, as I was rushing to get to an exam for one of my classes. He gave me his business card and told me to contact him if I needed anything. I thanked him and rushed to school carrying my broken bicycle.

After taking my exam, I met with my student advisor to tell him what had happened. He told me I should see a doctor and get checked for internal injuries. Taking his advice, I called the driver of the Mercedes, realizing, as I looked at his card, that he was one of the university's professors of criminal justice. When he answered the phone, I told him I was calling to take him up on his offer and wanted to get checked for injuries at a doctor.

His tone changed. He asked whether I thought the accident had been his fault and said we ought to meet at the local police station immediately. I agreed, realizing this couldn't be good.

Shortly after, we met as planned and I was brought into a small room with a bright incandescent lamp, much like the interrogation rooms I'd seen in American movies. The professor sat beside me while a police officer sat across from us both.

"Do you know what you've done, Mr. Prakash?"

I looked at him stunned and said I'd done nothing wrong. If he could show me an American law stating cars had the right of way over bikers and pedestrians, I would apologize. I also made it clear that though I may be an international student, I wasn't born yesterday.

I could tell from both men's body language they were taken aback but knew each other well and had every intention of trying to intimidate or fool me. Suddenly, the professor asked me a series of questions unrelated to the accident, attempting to bully me based on the color of my skin.

"Are you a Muslim?"

"Where are you from?"

"Are you Palestinian?"

"What's your religion?"

"Do you have health insurance?"

"Why did you come to the US?"

Rather than answering his questions, I replied that his racism couldn't be more transparent and advised him to check his arrogance. My pride in my familial roots and cultural upbringing had prepared me for encounters with men like him.

"You might think twice about how you spoke to me today, sir," I told him as I left the police station. "Someone like me could end up being your boss someday."

I not only stood up to those men that day but made sure that people around town knew what they'd done. I wrote a letter to the local newspaper detailing what had happened in a way that didn't name the professor directly but made clear who he was. The newspaper published it, and hundreds of people wrote to me in support, including the University of Idaho's Office of International Students.

LOCAL COMMENT

Faculty member's questions revealed his prejudices

By RAVI PRAKASH

On June 17, 1991, I met with a minor accident involving a University of Idaho faculty member. The accident involved my bike and his Mercedes.

I was not very concerned about the accident, but during the deliberation at the Moscow police station, this faculty member used words which were not at all in line with his profession and status in this community. I was emotionally disturbed by the incident and by the words used by this faculty member at the Moscow police station to describe me and all international students.

The following questions were asked in an attempt to intimidate me:

• Why are so many international students coming to the United States?

• Are you from Palestine?

• What is your religion?

• Who will pay your expenses?

All of this happened in front of a police officer. With due respect to other faculty members, here is what I have to tell him:

First of all, it's none of your business why I came to the U.S. There may be many reasons. Today we live in a global economy, whereby all of us are interlinked to each other. International students are an important part of this link.

Let me point out, that the majority of the international students are merit students and their first purpose is to finish their education. Immigrants from all over the world have contributed to the well-being of this country and the universities they attend.

We don't have to go back into the history to show the contribution of foreign-born people to this nation. Most Americans have their roots in foreign countries.

It seems to me that this faculty member does not understand the importance of international understanding and cooperation. When a foreign student returns to his/her home country, it can create enormous goodwill. This goodwill takes different shapes in the long run, e.g. in terms of better trade relationship, world peace through better understanding, and improved academic teaching, research, and extension, in other nations.

To me world peace and understanding are very precious. There is a lot more to gain by peace than by war. I hope this faculty member understands this. Building positive and meaningful relationships is important for the future. Stereotyped images of international students (and of each other) will not build a better world.

I was outraged when this faculty member asked me whether or not I was from Palestine, and what was my religion. English is my second language, but I understood what he meant by this remark.

This is deplorable behavior considering the fact that he is a teacher of criminal justice. He said that he had toured many countries, but that did not improve his prejudices. Not everyone in America is Caucasian, and so is true everywhere else in the world.

To infer that every Palestinian is a terrorist is a gross generalization. Religion, had nothing to do with what we were discussing at the police station. As someone from India, I have a much better understanding and tolerance for all religions than did this faculty member.

Finally, how I manage my expenses was not relevant to the accident. Like most native students, international students are not rich. Most survive on scholarships and grants, earned honestly. Most don't have any other source of income and are very cautious spenders. International students are in most part not allowed to work off-campus, except under certain special circumstances.

The faculty member had in his mind that I was at the police station to sue him and make money out of this accident. I am proud of my integrity and honesty, hopeful about the future, and I do not want to succeed at the expense of others. I felt during my conversation that this faculty member is very proud of being rich and powerful.

I would urge this faculty member to put himself in my shoes and see how he would have felt if the same thing had happened to him far away from his home. Yes, it's true that I don't like everything that goes on in this country and neither will he if he visits my home country. But, that is no excuse to abuse foreign students.

This episode exposed me to unnecessary prejudice. I hope this is my last such encounter. In spite of this, I will always be grateful to this nation for my education and shall always remember the good things that have happened to me. I hope this faculty member understands my point of view.

Ravi Prakash is a graduate student in the department of agricultural economics at the University of Idaho.

Ravi's letter to the newspaper

Later, the graduate faculty committee headed by the university chancellor invited me and the prejudiced professor to a meeting to discuss disciplinary action against him. Others told me I should sue. I was getting ready to defend my thesis, however, and was advised by a number of people to drop the matter. They didn't want my status as a student to suffer in case those judging my thesis happened to be friends with the professor.

In the end, I did let it go. My intention was never to destroy his or anyone else's career but to let the world know I would not be treated like a doormat. I had accomplished what I set out to do and set my sights back on my mission moving forward. From that experience, I learned firsthand of some people's willingness to take advantage of their fellow humans for their perceived weakness. It was a disappointing lesson, but I was proud to have kept my composure.

Throughout my two years in Idaho, I was laser focused on my studies and making good progress. In the fall of 1992, representatives from a bank in Washington state that catered to the agricultural community visited our campus to recruit jobseekers. I was selected as a finalist among their pool of applicants and invited for a series of interviews in Spokane. My professors in Idaho told me that the bank nearly always hired its finalists and, knowing my qualifications, were confident I would get the job.

Needless to say, I was excited to hear the news and did everything I could to prepare before my trip to Washington. I even borrowed money from a friend to buy a brand-new suit from the Burlington Coat Factory. The day of the interview was a cold December morning. I arrived early for a series of back-to-back interviews that ended with a conversation with the head of the bank. Everything went smoothly, and he asked me how soon I'd be able to start. I told him I'd be graduating in the summer of the following year and could start working immediately after. I just needed one thing from him: sponsorship for an H-1b visa.

Puzzled, the man looked at me and asked what that was.

"It's an employment visa all foreign nationals need to legally work full time in the US."

After eyeing me for a moment, he said he'd have the bank look into it, but I could tell he wasn't sincere. I finished the interview and walked to my car, passing the campus recruiter I'd met in Idaho on the way. She'd become a huge source of support and assured me I was a shoo-in for the job. She told me she'd be calling me shortly. I drove back to my university feeling hopeful but skeptical.

Back in Idaho, I settled in for the long wait to hear back from the bank, dreaming of what life would be like once I'd managed to begin my career. Not my next job, but my *career*.

Something I could pour my heart and soul into. Something with a good salary and benefits. Enough money not only to support myself, but a family in the future. I called Toyota, Nissan, and Honda, asking them to send me brochures for their newest cars, trying to convince myself I would be able to afford one sooner than later. No more rusted Malibu Classics for me. I was moving up in the world.

But as usual, life had a different plan for me, filled with new lessons to teach.

On Christmas Eve that year, I heard back from the kind bank recruiter in Washington, my biggest fan. She said she was sorry but that I didn't get the job, though she wasn't sure why. I would later find out my need for an H-1b visa had been a dealbreaker. The company had never had to deal with visas and could easily find a local candidate to fill the position rather than investing the time and money to bring me on board.

I was heartbroken. After hearing the news, I sat at my dining room table across from Bill, who could feel the gravity of the situation. Tears flowed down my cheeks, and I asked what I would have to do to finally prove myself to the world. I tore up the car brochures and did what I usually did when the path forward was hazy: I went for a run, strategizing about my next move.

I had eight months to figure out what I could do after graduation to avoid becoming an illegal immigrant. Getting another master's degree (number three, if you've been counting) was an option. Rather than continuing to study agriculture, I decided to switch fields and focus on getting an MBA, hoping stronger business qualifications might open some doors and jumpstart my career. I applied to ten programs, begging several of them to waive the application fee. Luckily, a few obliged.

In July 1992, I was accepted with a teaching assistantship to the University of North Carolina in Charlotte. I was elated to have a new solution to my visa issue but stressed about the precarious loop I was stuck in. It had been four years since I'd moved to America, and there had been challenges around every corner. Financially speaking, I was beyond broke. Mentally and emotionally, I was exhausted.

But I wouldn't give up. There was never a doubt about that.

I would need a car to drive to my new school in Charlotte, as I had sold my 8-cylinder 1977 Blue Malibu Classic after arriving in Moscow. As I was looking into my options, some friends brought to my attention that my old car was on the market for $75. However, given the price of the gas and my tight budget (ZERO dollars), buying it back could be no more than a pipe dream. I relayed my disappointment to Bill at home, who sympathized after witnessing two years of my financial struggles and visa issues.

During the first week of August, I invited my advisor, Dr. Joel Gunther, and all my classmates to my apartment for lunch. I made a small feast from inexpensive ingredients like lentils, rice, garbanzo beans, and salad, while Bill pitched in with desserts and snacks. Around twenty people showed up, and I thanked them all for their friendship and the wonderful memories I would carry with me for the rest of my life. I was truly sad to be leaving Idaho. I had fallen in love with the Northwest.

When it was time to leave, my advisor and friends thanked me in return and handed me an envelope full of cash—$165 total. They'd all intuited that I had no money to help me get to Charlotte, even though I had a position waiting for me there. I thanked them profusely for their kindness, generosity, and support.

A few days later, Bill drove me to Spokane so I could rent a brand-new Malibu Classic (yes, the same model as before!) one-way to Charlotte. He helped pay for the rental, and I loaded it up before hugging him with a heavy heart. With that, I said goodbye to yet another friend and was on the road again, heading southeast. I felt nowhere close to carefree like I had during the drive from Wisconsin to Idaho. I was determined but discouraged, imagining what I'd have to do if I still couldn't land a good job after getting an MBA. What then?

University of Life

LESSON #5: FAILURE AND DISAPPOINTMENT

Our letdowns serve as clever guides that keep us humble and hungry. We can prevent succumbing to self-victimization by assigning meaning related to resourcefulness to our setbacks. Without life's curveballs, we often remain stuck, trapped in the invisible prison of our comfort zone. How have failure and disappointment helped you grow?

SIX

On the Grind in Charlotte

"Obstacles don't have to stop you. If you run into a wall, don't turn around and give up. Figure out how to climb it, go through it, or work around it."

—Michael Jordan, basketball legend

I was back at square one again, or at least that's how it felt. I had no money, aside from the $165 from my teachers and friends in Idaho, another degree on the horizon to earn, and absolutely no guarantees about my future. I set out on the next leg of my adventure toward Charlotte, North Carolina, desperately believing with everything I had left that things would work out as long as I didn't give up.

There was no rush to arrive in North Carolina. I took around a week to drive there, just as I had when I left Wisconsin for Idaho, taking that time to reflect, recharge, and rewire myself for another period of uncertainty. Again, I slept in my car at rest areas and parking lots but couldn't afford to take many detours. I needed every penny I had for gas, food, and the future.

At some point while driving through South Dakota, I encountered a group of thousands of motorcyclists on their way to the Sturgis Motorcycle Rally. At first, the sight of them all fascinated me, but the situation turned dangerous when a group of them surrounded my car and kept me boxed in for upwards of an hour. I had heard there were pockets of white supremacist activity in the region and didn't want to risk provoking any bikers who might subscribe to such beliefs. Needless to say, I did my best to keep a safe distance and avoid hitting them, constantly keeping an eye out for a chance to free myself. At the first opportunity I got, I floored it out of there. Unfortunately, I'd only made it a few miles ahead when a cop pulled me over for speeding.

The officer began as cops usually do, asking me my name and where I was from. I told him I was from India, and he asked what county that was in, apparently not realizing I was referring to an entirely different *country*. Rather than correcting him, I told him India was north of a county in Idaho I was familiar with. He seemed to buy it and asked if I knew why he'd stopped me. I told him I understood he'd stopped me for speeding and tried to give him my excuse, but he didn't buy *that* and wrote me a ticket for $60. I had to pay it there and then, as I wouldn't be able to go back to South Dakota to deal with it later.

Getting back on the road, I knew I'd just gotten myself into another financial bind. I would have to take the shortest route possible to Charlotte to avoid running out of cash. There was no GPS or help from Google Maps in those days. All I had was a paper map to guide my way. I did my best to drive at the legal speed and avoid running out of gas. I only ate when necessary and drank nothing but water, used to dancing with hunger over the last four years.

I made it to Charlotte with $5 dollars left in my pocket and went straight to the office for international students. Fortunately, the staff there had a list of students who had offered to host people like me short term while I searched for more permanent accommodations. I connected with a group of Indian graduate students who were gracious enough to let me stay with them for a couple weeks. They never asked me for any money. I felt guilty about not being able to contribute to the grocery fund they used to cook elaborate dinners at the house, but I needed to keep my $5 dollars. It was all I had left to my name.

To avoid mooching off my hosts too much, I would leave the house first thing in the morning with a change of clothes and go to campus so I could shower and shave there. I would scrounge bits of leftover food to eat while no one was looking, usually at one of the cafeterias or events where food was sold. The situation wasn't great, but I made it work.

With everything else going on in my life, my lack of food was far from my biggest concern. I needed to settle in and find a means of surviving.

It would be a month before I would receive my first paycheck from the school for my teaching assistantship. My $5 dollar bill certainly wouldn't suffice while I searched for a roommate and a long-term living arrangement. I reached out to Dr. Maski in Wisconsin, who had lent me money many times and was kind enough to help me once more.

I ended up staying in the dorms that first semester, as it would be an easy way to meet people. My resident advisor came to me and asked if I would agree to be roommates with a guy called Trevor. Trevor had Parkinson's disease and always shook as a result. For this reason, no one would room with him, but I accepted without hesitation. He was exceptionally smart and well read. We would watch presidential debates together and get into fascinating conversations about politics. At one point, he suggested I find a nice American girl to marry for a visa, which others before him had brought up many times, but I refused. I eventually learned that Trevor's family wasn't supportive of him and had taken him off their health insurance plan. One time, he broke his foot and had no way of getting help to pay his medical bills. I'm not sure how he got by in the end, but watching his situation from the outside left a terrible taste in my mouth.

I was disturbed by the American healthcare system and how good people like Trevor were left to fend for themselves.

After one semester in the dorms, I decided to move off campus. I found a room in a house with another group of students and began thinking about how I would support myself over the summer, as my assistantship would (again) not be covering those months. I attended a seminar for students seeking internships. We weren't allowed to contact employers ourselves—the staff at the office told us they would send out our applications and get back to us. In the end, everyone who attended the seminar got an internship except me. At that point, I was already struggling to pay my bills on time, and the question of how I would survive had me desperate.

In a dress shirt and tie, I walked all over Charlotte applying to any part-time job that would accept applications. One day, I went back to the internship office and spoke to the administrative assistant there to ask if I could see my file. During the seminar, we had to submit around twenty resumes printed on thick, watermarked paper. To my shock, all the ones I had submitted were still in the file. The office hadn't sent out a single one in my name as they had promised.

Furious, I barged into the office of the Director of Career Services, who had told me employers weren't interested in hiring international students, which was why I hadn't been hired.

I threw my file on the table. "Explain this to me."

She looked up, stunned, asking what the problem was.

"I was told," I said, practically breathing fire, "that employers wouldn't be interested in hiring me, yet none of you have even tried to help. You didn't send out a single resume I submitted."

She tried to tell me the resumes in the file were photocopies, but the watermarks on the documents showed through when I held them against the light, exposing her lie. She didn't admit to her wrongdoing, but I had caught her, and she knew it.

After that, I visited one of the international student advisors, who had always been extremely helpful. Incensed, I explained what was going on.

"Ravi, you should go and speak with the university chancellor. This is wrong."

It was wrong, but I knew the woman at the internship office would be fired if I truly made a fuss. I didn't want that weight on my conscience. Instead, after sleeping on it, I went back to her office, left her with a couple of the resumes from my file, and told her to find me an internship immediately. If she refused to help, I would report her.

I left and continued my search, taking my other resumes with me. Tired of walking in the sun in my dress shirt and dress shoes, drenched with sweat, I stopped at Charlotte's biggest mall, which had an ice-skating rink. I sat down to rest, grateful for the cool air, when a man sat down next to me and asked what I was doing there.

"I'm looking for a job and came here to rest. I'm a graduate student at UNCC."

He pointed at the jewelry store across from us and told me he was the manager there, and that he was looking for an assistant. I told him I'd be thrilled to take the opportunity.

"What do you know about jewelry?" he asked me.

"Well, I know gold is yellow and silver is white."

"Do you know there's also white gold?"

"I do now."

We both laughed, and he gave me an application, urging me to fill it out.

"Look," I told him, "I'm an international student. I need permission from my school to work for you."

"Whatever you need," he said, "just let me know. We'll figure it out."

That man's name was Robert Cuillare. He was a Mexican-American from Texas and therefore understood my situation, able to sympathize with how hard life in America could be for immigrants.

With a job finally in hand, I went back to the internship office and told the woman there I needed permission to take on a paid internship as an assistant manager at the jewelry shop. She was either going to give me that permission or lose her job for how she'd discriminated against me. She hesitated, but ultimately approved my plan, and I was legally hired, finally able to get my first H1-B visa in the process and put the MBA on hold. Exhausted, I began working, intent on paying back all my debts and getting back to my normal self.

Working at the jewelry store required some initial investment. I needed to buy several suits and a car to help me drive to and from work. I found a used Toyota Corolla that would cost around $2,000 dollars, meaning I would need to take out another loan. I went to United Carolina bank and spoke with a woman named Brenda. After telling her about my situation, she said she couldn't grant me the loan because I had nothing to offer as collateral.

"My word is my collateral, Brenda," I insisted.

"Anyone can say that, Mr. Prakash. We don't just hand out loans."

Although I had a lot of debt at the time, I also had great credit history because I made all my minimum payments on time. Brenda shared with me that the repayment rate on loans to immigrants at their bank was around ninety percent, far higher than the local population.

"Look, Brenda, I will be among that ninety percent. I'm not asking for a million dollars. I'm asking for $2,000 and will pay it off long before the amount is due."

We talked for nearly an hour and a half. Finally, Brenda went to talk with her superior at the bank and came back with a smile on her face. "Okay, Mr. Prakash. I'll grant you the loan."

Elated, I bought the Toyota Corolla and started working seven days a week, not taking a single day off for about a year. Little by little, I began paying everyone back—Dr. Maski, the bank, and everyone else who had helped me out. Soon after, however, the car started giving me problems. It turned out to be a lemon I couldn't afford to fix.

Again, I needed another loan but this time was able to get one relatively easily thanks to the relationships I had built.

I called Carol, a loan officer at Latha Credit Union in Moscow, Idaho. She and I had first met in the fall of 1990 in Idaho. She had moved there from Wisconsin, which gave us some common ground to work with. Throughout my two years in Idaho, Carol had helped me with a number of small loans, which I'd promptly paid off. When I called from Charlotte, she didn't hesitate to process my car loan and help me out. I got a reliable Honda Accord with only 20,000 miles on it, which I ended up driving for twenty-seven years, only making the move to replace it in 2016.

Life at the jewelry store was never boring. A whole range of people would come in, some of whom were nice. Others, however, were unbelievably arrogant. One gentleman who came by wanted to look at two Rolex watches at a time, which we weren't advised to let customers do. I asked to see his ID, and he scoffed, "Do you know who I am?!"

He was apparently an administrator at the local sports franchise, but that mattered little to me. I was done with his attitude.

"I don't care who you are. I'm following the law, which says I can ask you to show your identification." I pointed his attention to a printout that said the exact same thing, attached at one corner of the display.

"I know the owner of this store."

"That's fine. You want to call him? I'll give you the phone."

He walked out pissed off with his embarrassed wife on his arm.

On another day, a man in a hoodie walked in and asked to look at a Rolex Presidential watch. Immediately, I got the sense something was off. Like the sports administrator, he asked to see two watches at once, but I knew I couldn't hand them to him. I held them both in my hands tightly in order to show them to him, but in a split second, he snatched them and ran.

I pursued the thief, but Robert ran after me and told me not to chase him, seeing as he might have had a gun. I followed his order but was afraid of what would happen next. I had just lost the store twenty grand and didn't earn nearly enough to cover the cost. Thankfully, the owners of the company were exceptionally good people and told me not to worry about it. They had insurance and told me never to chase any thieves who came through.

The majority of our customers either didn't realize or didn't appreciate how difficult working there was.

Imagine standing on your feet for ten to fourteen hours a day. Holidays were the worst. We had practically no time to even eat or take bathroom breaks. Due to my financial situation, I signed up for any and all extra hours I could find. If someone took a day off, I would volunteer to cover.

I learned a lot about human behavior and relationships there. We'd have couples come in who jointly made upwards of half a million dollars, but when we ran their credit history, they couldn't even afford our $10 dollar watches. Others would come in who had dated for ten years and one would tell the other right in front of us, "You buy me that ring today or get out of my life."

I worked hard and was always one of the top ten salespeople out of 125 stores, but my approach was worlds away from that of a typical sales guy. I was upfront with people. If a client wanted my feedback on their purchase, they would get my honest opinion regardless of how it might affect the sale.

"Be authentic, be willing to take the road less traveled if neces-sary, and be willing to stay connected to your core."

—Rumi, poet, theologian, and scholar

I had paused my MBA program to work full time and try to pay off my loans.

In 1994, I finally managed to do so and was determined to finish my degree. I would need yet another loan to complete the program, so I applied to borrow $40,000 dollars from Citibank, which required paperwork about my courses from my university. My school failed to send those papers, letting me down again, which meant I couldn't start my courses on time and lost yet another year in Charlotte working at the jewelry store. The following year, I applied again, this time with the sponsorship of the friend of my dad's boss who had originally granted me $2,000 when I came to America. But the loan was denied.

Frustrated, I asked for help from a college friend from India named Osler Kamat. He had been a year ahead of me during my undergraduate, went on to graduate from Virginia Tech, and had recently found a job in Florida. He had secured a green card by then and agreed to be a cosigner on my loan application. I remember writing him a letter.

To whom it may concern,

I, Ravi Prakash, acknowledge that I am only asking Osler to sign this so I can get the student loan. I will be solely responsible to pay back the debt in full. If due to some unforeseen reason, I am not able to fulfill my commitment, all of my assets can be sold to pay off the debt.

My intentions were good, and Osler knew that, but the only assets I had at the time were 145 boxes of books, files, notebooks, and old computers. I doubt they would have been worth anything near the $40,000 in loans I had applied for. It was our trust as students that we had built while attending school in India that carried the day. Eventually, after a lot of phone calls and persistence with a staff member from the bank, I was able to get the loan granted.

My financial drama didn't end there. When the loan was approved, it was sent to my school in Charlotte, which was then responsible for releasing the funds to me. When I went to the university in 1995, they told me they weren't holding any money there in my name, despite the fact that I had confirmation from the bank. I had to kick up a huge fuss with the vice president of finance on campus.

"What's going on here?" I asked. "This is not your money. It's my money. It's my debt, and you can't deny it to me."

Eventually, I got the issue sorted and quit my job at the jewelry store, switching back to an F-1 student visa in the fall of 1995.

Within a couple of days of returning to school, while I was sitting in the cafeteria enjoying a cup of tea, another guy from India sat down and began talking to me. He was also enrolled in the MBA program and, much to both of our surprise, had a connection through our families. Our dads had both worked together at the fertilizer plant back in Sindri.

We had lived a block away from each other for many years, totally unaware we would meet years later on the other side of the world.

As it turned out, he was living with his sister and brother-in-law in town, who owned a bustling travel agency. He introduced me to them, and we hit it off from the get-go. The brother-in-law was looking for someone to manage his back office at the agency and asked if I would be interested. Able to work legally for up to twenty hours per week as an intern, I said yes, and he showed me the place. It was a busy, messy business lacking organization. I told the brother-in-law that as long as he could be flexible and work around my university schedule, I could fulfill the role.

My classes lasted from 6:00 p.m. to 9:00 p.m. during the week. I would get out of school, go to the travel agency, take care of the back office from 10:00 p.m. to 4:00 a.m., sleep for a couple of hours, go for a run, work out, cook, eat, do my homework, and get ready to go to school at 6:00 p.m. Zero room to breathe.

From fall of 1995 through August 1997, every second of my life was accounted for. It was exhausting, but I remember feeling fulfilled in a strange way, having grown up watching everyone in my family work nonstop. I functioned like a well-oiled machine, unhindered by internal obstacles. One of the first questions I asked my new boss was how much money his business made. He told me he didn't quite know.

"How can you not know?"

"All I know," he said, "is that I pay my bills on time."

Right away, I could tell the business was likely in dire straits. He was a wholesale seller of airline tickets, and his clients were other travel agencies, retail customers, and corporate clients. The problem was that he was too nice, allowing people to book tickets without paying for them at the time of issue. This happened so often that my boss was paying exorbitant amounts in overdraft fees on his account, which he wasn't fully aware of. I also figured out some shipping companies were charging him two or three times for a single transaction. In short order, I helped him get his ducks in a row, denying customers tickets unless they were willing to pay in full immediately. By doing this, I ensured he never paid another cent in overdraft fees. I also updated his travel brochures, some of which were ten years old.

Just like at the jewelry store, life at the travel agency was never dull. One customer wanted to go to Texas, but couldn't tell us where, so we eventually sold her a ticket to Houston and hoped for the best. Another showed up one day to check in for her flight, insisting we were responsible for checking her in because we had sold her the ticket. Nothing was going to change her mind, so I drove her to the airport, where she finally understood how the process worked.

Around sixty percent of our client base at the agency was made up of second-generation immigrants, many of whom were searching for a "suitable boy" for their daughters to marry. They would call or stop by the office and ask all sorts of questions to indirectly suss out whether I might be a viable candidate. If I passed their test, they would drop hints more directly, telling me marriage could solve my visa issues. I could indeed get permanent residency or citizenship if I were to marry a US citizen. Many times, I'd go along with their questions for fun, seeing how far they were willing to take the conversation.

Of course, I'd never marry anyone whose family had tried to buy my loyalty, but it made my days more interesting.

Finally, the time to graduate came, and for my final project, I had to do a group project involving an actual business in town. My colleagues and I had to advise a brand-new community bank and help its staff come up with a five-year plan. They needed creative ideas for how to track competing businesses and differentiate themselves in a tight banking market. As luck would have it, our contact at that bank ended up being none other than Brenda, the woman who had granted me the car loan in 1993. We were thrilled to see each other, reuniting with an instant bond of trust.

My group and I discussed several ideas but went with the one I proposed. Going off my personal experience of having trouble getting a loan, I suggested that we come up with a survey of all the businesses owned by immigrants in Charlotte to learn about their experience raising capital. I wanted to know how easy or difficult it was for them to get business loans.

We gathered a wealth of valuable data and eventually presented our plan to the board of Brenda's bank. It was well received, and one of the men, who happened to be the founder of the bank and an industry legend in Charlotte, pulled me aside to invite me out to dinner at a revolving restaurant in town.

From atop the tower, we had a panoramic view of the city that slowly turned 360 degrees as we ate. I'd never been to such a fancy spot, and everyone there was all dressed up, unlike me. We had a long conversation, and I soon realized he was offering me a job at the bank, impressed by the work I had done. I thanked him profusely, expressing my gratitude but turned down his offer. Charlotte hadn't been particularly good to me, and I didn't want to stay. I had never felt welcome, or that I belonged there.

I knew I was making the right decision, but it felt like a waste considering the struggle I'd gone through to find a career-level job.

All the applications and rejection letters. All the time I'd spent waiting to hear back. All the loans, debt, stress, and begging for help. It was also one of the first times someone in the business world recognized me as a fellow human being and appreciated what my team and I had done for them. I will always be grateful for that moment in my life. It raised my hope, albeit slightly, that there might be a light at the end of the tunnel.

In July 1996, I took a road trip to Atlanta, Georgia, to watch the summer Olympics with a friend named Mike, an amateur comedian I'd worked with at the jewelry store. We had an incredible time, not sleeping for a full two days due to our unbridled excitement. People in the city were on their best behavior for the event, and I left with sparkles in my eyes, in love with the city and its people.

Back in Charlotte, before graduation, I had a single class remaining before I could finish my MBA. As luck would have it, I discovered I could take the class at Mercer University in Atlanta. I had also begun hearing about a software company called Oracle, which offered a certification course there that could lead to professional opportunities. I enrolled, paying the $700 dollar fee with no idea where or how I'd be able to live there.

Ravi at his graduation at UNC-Charlotte, MBA program with Mike from the jewelry store and Ed, classmate from the MBA program

I was immensely lucky to meet a woman who worked at the Oracle Training Center, who told me she would be gone during the summer. She offered to let me stay at her place, provided I took care of the house and paid the utilities. It was a steal, so I went for it, even though I still had my apartment in Charlotte. I drove back and forth between there and Atlanta, juggling my responsibilities in both places.

All in all, my five years in Charlotte were incredibly hard. Still, I'm thankful, as my time there revealed who I was becoming and what I was able to overcome. This brought out the best traits I possessed and encouraged me to refine them.

Though I hadn't yet broken into the corporate world, I was beginning to trust I would soon. My element of faith caused me to turn down the job offer at the bank in Charlotte and make the move to Atlanta.

Truth be told, I was quickly approaching the end of my runway, on the precipice of a cliff's edge. I would have to make things work for myself in my new home or move back to India, unable to finish the journey I had started. There was no way I was going to attend yet another school and start the study cycle all over again. The time had come to make my next big leap. I just needed the universe to show me the way forward.

University of Life

LESSON #6: MAINTAINING MOMENTUM

To accomplish goals and make our impact, we must ensure that we keep moving forward, relentlessly putting one foot in front of the other. Whether we're carrying out menial tasks or leading large teams, constant movement is key to success. How do you maintain your momentum?

SEVEN

Laundry-Room Breakthroughs

"Success is not final, failure is not fatal. It is the courage to continue that counts."

—Winston Churchill, former United Kingdom prime minister

I left Charlotte for Atlanta in 1997, determined never to return. Based on my two-day trip with my friend Mike during the Olympics, I had a gut feeling my new city would open doors for me. The energy had been warm, and the people there had been helpful. I looked forward, especially, to the Oracle training and certification course, looking to align myself with the software industry's newest darling.

There was no room for failure. I had just enough money to last me until the end of the year, provided I continued to live like a penniless graduate student. Friends would invite me out, but my tight budget prevented me from joining them, and as always, I would provide excuses for turning them down.

My head was exploding at the time. I was facing the very real possibility of needing to return to India without ever landing an opportunity to earn decent money and turn my situation around. I had accumulated about $100,000 dollars in debt from my loans from Citibank, credit card companies, and friends. Nearly everyone who knew about my situation was betting this would be the year I would have to return home. Some even encouraged me to leave without taking care of my debts, but I was determined to pay everyone back.

My love of exercise and plant-based food kept me fit and clear headed, allowing me to block out the noise of stress. I finally finished my remaining MBA class and the Oracle course while building my network in Atlanta. Around that time, the IT job market was exploding across the country. People were moving from all over the world to work in the US, which meant more companies were becoming acquainted with H-1b visas and how they worked. The fact that I was an immigrant was slowly becoming less of a liability.

Knowing what I knew about finances, I calculated I'd be able to survive in Atlanta until the end of February of the following year without a job. My house-sitting gig was up, so I started looking for an apartment, which helped me get familiar with the city. I wrote an ad in *Creative Loafing* magazine looking for two roommates to share an apartment with. Over the next several days, the responses I got overwhelmed me, and I'd come home to endless messages on my answering machine. Most were from random folks who seemed more interested in dating rather than becoming my housemate. There was one person, however, a student named Mary, who was pursuing a PhD in clinical psychology. I told her to come to check out an apartment with me the next morning, and she agreed.

I immediately pulled my ad out of the magazine, sick of the phone calls, and visited the Emory University housing office to see if I could find another potential housemate. There was a woman there with her mother looking for a place, and I asked if they'd be interested in house-hunting with me and Mary. Our budgets aligned, and they had no objection to sharing an apartment with a man.

The next morning, the three ladies showed up on time, and I prepared a delicious breakfast for us to share before we drove around to check out the apartments I had researched. My hard work paid off quickly. We found a brand-new apartment with three bedrooms and two bathrooms. We were all elated and relieved to have a guarantee of a roof over our heads.

It was a good omen. After nine years in America maybe, just maybe, the stars would finally align for me.

A week after moving into the apartment, I met a neighbor named Peter while doing my laundry at the complex. We got to talking, and he casually asked what I was doing in Atlanta. Upon hearing I was searching for a job, he asked if I would pass my resume along to him, promising to recommend me to his superiors. He worked for a telecommunications company located close to where we were living. I had never been particularly interested in telecommunications but found the advances I was seeing in phone technology fascinating, especially as someone who had to pay exorbitant fees just to call my family. The offer piqued my interest, and within a week; I was invited to attend a series of interviews and landed my first professional job with a big company. I was suddenly making a salary of $45,000 per year and gave myself permission to buy new clothes, shoes, and a camera.

"Sometimes the greatest adventure is simply a conversation."

—Unknown

The reality of $100,000 of debt in my name was still a burden. It was all I could think about. As always, my visa issues accompanied my financial situation. I was going to work at the telecom company with a year-long work permit for international students. If I did well and the company decided to keep employing me, it would have to apply for an H-1b visa in my name, ensuring a more permanent role for me.

Unfortunately, within my first week there, it was clear that the business culture was a mismatch.

In virtually all of my public speaking gigs these days, I start by saying energy is everything, and I mean it. One cannot do anything in life without energy, and this place sucked the energy right out of me. I shared an area with five other people who would rarely speak, even with me. I sensed the majority of the folks around me were there to make money and lacked the usual human touch most of us expect of each other.

All of this reminded me of Charlotte. I had moved to Atlanta in search of something more emotionally satisfying, so I sat down with my manager and told him I wanted to resign. He nearly fell out of his chair, not believing that someone right out of college with so much debt would throw such an opportunity away. He took me outside for a walk and urged me to be patient, advising me to take more time to learn the job and make my decision. I took his advice, but deep down, I knew I would be moving on as soon as possible. I had worked so many jobs I hated over the previous nine years that I was determined by then to work somewhere inspiring.

Out of sheer coincidence, I was once again doing my laundry a few weeks later and met another neighbor, Sampath. We started talking, and he told me he, like Peter, was working for a telecommunications company too. He asked if I was interested in traveling internationally.

"Traveling to where?" I asked.

"Brazil."

As it turned out, Sampath worked for a German telecom startup that sold enterprise software worldwide for customer care and billing. I knew very little about Brazil, but my instincts told me to be open to his offer. He asked for my resume, and within a couple weeks they offered me the position starting in April 1998. In March, I resigned from my energy-sucking job, looking forward to the future. Upon hiring me, my new employer helped me begin the process of applying for an H-1b and subsequently for a green card. I would finally be able to obtain permanent residency and resolve my visa issues once and for all.

After a week of training at my new job, I was invited to a kick-off meeting for a new project. There, I sat next to Janet, the project director, and across from a man named Rajul, along with several other coworkers. I was nervous, having come from a nontechnical background. From what I understood, I was expected to do what was called "business configuration" for the company's system. Having no idea what that meant, I later reached out to Rajul to introduce myself and ask if he understood what we were supposed to do. He had a computer science background and assured me our tasks would be fairly straightforward.

From that day onward, he spent several months teaching me about the company's system, SQL, and UNIX after everyone else left the office.

Many days, I wouldn't return home until three a.m. Eventually, I could configure the entire system without error. I was even able to start teaching and mentoring new employees, which elevated my reputation and influence in the company.

During this initial period in Atlanta, I used to see a runner pass my apartment each day. Being a runner myself, I became increasingly curious about his routine. How far was he running? Where did he go? Out of the blue one day, I followed him on his route in my car, careful not to bother or freak him out, and realized he had run about ten miles altogether. Having never run more than three or four miles at a time, his self-discipline inspired me.

The next day, I laced up my running shoes and ran the same ten-mile loop without stopping. I was stunned by what I was able to do in the heat of the Atlanta summer and began running that ten-mile loop three to four times a week. Thanks to that training, I later won a 10k course organized by my company. Though I didn't know it at the time, this habit was setting me up for a long future of marathon running.

Back at work, six months after I was hired, my company opened a Latin American division in Miami. Our senior vice president in Atlanta was appointed to move there. I initiated a conversation with him one day and he selected me, along with five other people, to move to Miami and join the new division. The time had apparently come to uproot myself once more, though I had a job in hand this time. Toward the end of 1998, I arrived in Miami with all my ducks in a row. My company had even applied for my coveted H-1b visa.

Before I could settle in Miami, I had to travel outside of the country to get a stamp on my passport and finalize my work visa. I could have gone to Mexico or Canada, but I followed my heart and instead asked my company to send me to Brazil so I could get a taste of the culture, not knowing how that decision would transform my future. Knowing they might send me there to work in the future, my boss approved my request, and I landed in Sao Paulo on a direct flight.

> It had rained on my way there, and the air smelled of fresh moisture as I left the plane. While waiting for the taxi to my hotel, it was as if someone was talking to my soul, telling me this was where I belonged.

The ambiance was a bit like India's, with an airport that was simple, straightforward, and full of commotion. After catching my cab, we drove forty minutes to my hotel. I didn't speak a word of Portuguese and the driver spoke no English, but we managed to talk in a broken mishmash of languages. He was a good sport about it.

The staff at the hotel—the Crowne Plaza Hotel on Paulista Avenue, the Manhattan of Brazil—were friendly and welcoming, though the language barrier was an issue. On the way to the US Consulate to get my passport stamp, I found a corner store across the street that made fresh smoothies and juices. It was heaven. Finally, I had access to my favorite foods, and they weren't even expensive! I drank one glass after another, enamored with everything I'd seen so far.

At the consulate, I stood in line and met a student from Colombia who had studied civil engineering in the US. We hit it off, and he told me he lived and worked locally. Knowing I didn't have much time in Sao Paulo, he offered to show me around town. I accepted, not knowing whether he was sincere or trying to scam me but going with the flow, regardless. He seemed honest enough, and I was relaxed, open, and ready for a life away from the stressful life of the previous nine years.

He picked me up from my hotel later on, drove me around the city, and showed me the sights. First, we went to a fancy mall named Morumbi where an Indian festival was happening, but the revelers were mostly Brazilian. It was an eye-opener for me to see non-Indians celebrating with so much love for my country.

I also went on walks alone at night while I was there, having no idea about the security situation. At one point, I heard music and figured it was coming from a club. I walked in and people were dancing, but when I tried to get a glass of water, no one would serve me. Eventually, I figured out I'd strolled into a private party of physicians who didn't care to speak with me because I looked different, being the only person of color. That left a bad taste in my mouth, but the next day I ventured out again, this time finding a real club. Again, everything was decorated in Indian artifacts, and I found out the owner loved my country very much. He would travel to India every year and spend stretches of time there.

The next day, I was walking and decided to stop in at a nice coffee shop. I've never been a coffee drinker but felt a pull to check the place out, as Brazil is world renowned for its coffee. Inside, there were three large painted murals, all of which portrayed scenes from Indian mythology. I had no means of asking the people there about them, so I simply sat and admired the art as I sipped my drink. It felt like an omen. The universe was speaking to me.

Soon, a woman and her granddaughter sat across from me at the cafe. Somehow, we got to talking, and I realized the grandmother spoke English. We talked for an hour or two. She was a local who lived nearby. They both took me around and showed me the whole neighborhood, explaining as I asked questions. When we'd finished, she gave me her phone number and told me to contact her if I ever needed anything. Brazil was full of kind folks willing to show me around. Later on, I also met a group of young people who brought me with them to check out the music cafes before dropping me back at my hotel.

I ended my first trip to Brazil with a phenomenal impression of the country and its people.

A message had been sent to my subconscious: Brazil was meant for me and wanted me there.

That feeling has never left my heart and to this day, just thinking of Brazil makes me want to be there.

Looking back on my previous nine years of struggle, I realized how much of my success had stemmed from my willingness to put myself out there. There was no time or space to be shy about my situation. I couldn't afford to be introverted or wait for luck to find me. I had to go out and talk to everyone I could in order to find the rare gems who would help me. I certainly had never expected my big break would happen in a laundry room, but as we know, *inflection points* often come in small, subtle packages.

What choice do we have in life but to try our best?

If we want to succeed, we have to keep going when life gets hard, and there's no way around that. I didn't just come to America to prove I could make it. There was more beneath the surface that I had only begun to build awareness around. I wanted to support my parents back in India. I wanted to support my sisters and their families. I wanted to be able to lend or give money to everyone I cared about, just as so many people had done for me throughout my journey. Once all was said and done and I had launched my career in telecommunications, the lessons I had learned from the University of Life were priceless, and the people I'd formed relationships with would stay in my heart forever. I had sown the seeds of a promising future throughout my years of struggle. The time had come to start reaping my harvest.

If I can pass along one lesson from that period, it's this: Get out there. Do your laundry! See what the world has to offer you. You never know who you're going to meet.

University of Life

LESSON #7: ONE CONVERSATION

A single conversation has the power to alter the trajectory of our journey, weaving whole new paths for us to travel. Actively seeking out conversations with those around us, whether known and unknown, can deliver the game-changing moment we seek. What was one conversation that changed your life?

EIGHT

Love Reveals Itself

"The heart wants what it wants, or else it does not care."

—Emily Dickinson

Shortly after moving to Miami, I was asked to visit Mexico City on a fact-finding mission for a software implementation project that was going badly. There were major communication problems within the team, and they needed a strong leader to hold people accountable. I was still new to the company and had no hands-on project experience, but the senior vice president of our Latin American division had confidence in my abilities. He asked me to come up with recommendations on how to turn the project around. I was nervous but focused on observing, listening, understanding, and asking questions. After two weeks, I had formed my recommendations, which were well received by both my VP and our client in Mexico. I got a stamp of approval indicating I could deliver in my professional sphere.

Toward the end of 1998, a request came in for someone who could work for a month on a project in Campinas, Brazil. I had an academic understanding of the subject matter, so my name was proposed. My excitement was through the roof. There was something about the idea of working there that spoke to me, though I didn't quite know what that "something" was yet.

Ravi with his team in Campinas, Brazil, in 1999

I arrived in Campinas on New Year's Eve. To my surprise, the hotel my company had booked me into was unimpressive and had no food I could eat. On January 1, everything was closed, so I had to manage on nothing but water. The next day, I was able to move to the Naomi Plaza Hotel next door. There, they offered an incredible Brazilian breakfast packed with fresh fruit and juices, which I devoured. Right up my alley.

Upon arriving at work, I sat down with two of my immediate supervisors, a young man from Switzerland and another from England. I told them I was nervous, given my lack of experience with the software system. They both assured me they were available to help with anything I needed. I was thrilled to be working on such an international team. We had folks on that project from around twenty countries.

Within two weeks, I was told I'd be able to work there through the end of 1999. My month-long offer had been extended to a year, and I grabbed the bull by the horns, accepting immediately. I poured my time and energy into learning, growing, and delivering results. I also formed fantastic relationships.

Making friends was easy in Brazil. People were outgoing and happy-go-lucky, always having fun and offering their help.

One Friday night in May 1999, two coworkers from Malaysia and I decided to take a weekend trip to the nearby city of Rio de Janeiro. We arrived there at 3 a.m., the sight of Copacabana Beach and the sound of crashing waves causing us to bubble with excitement. We checked into our hotel and walked straight out to the sand. I carried my tripods and a couple of high-end cameras and lenses to capture the moment. I can say with certainty that ignorance was bliss in that moment. No sane person with knowledge of the situation in Rio would venture onto the beach there in the middle of the night with such expensive goods in hand, but we had no idea.

Ravi with friends in Rio De Janeiro, May 1999

We stayed until dawn, taking pictures until the sun rose, and the full spectacle of Rio's beauty engulfed me. It was only my second time ever on a beach. The first had been in Goa as an undergraduate, and while I'd seen the beach in Miami, the energy there hadn't drawn me in. A desire to run in the sand overcame me. Life often grants us many things we take for granted, and this incredible beach was prompting me to immerse myself in the moment in order to make the most of it. I returned to the hotel with my friends, who wanted to sleep and rest, and dropped off my equipment before returning to the beach alone in my running shoes.

Out on the beach, I started running on the uneven sand, which I wasn't used to. Within minutes, I felt sudden, excruciating pain in both my knees and collapsed. Tears streamed down my cheeks as I imagined the worst, thinking I might never be able to run again. Luckily, my two friends saw me fall from our hotel room and came running out to pick me up. I limped back with them and somehow found the strength to shower and freshen up. We only had the weekend to see the city, and I didn't want to waste our chance. I limped around the city all Saturday and Sunday before driving all night with my friends so we could get back to the office on Monday.

Back at work, I asked around for recommendations, telling everyone I needed to see a specialist in orthopedics to help me fix my knees. A friend of mine, Kassia Costa, whose sister was a doctor, found one and made me an appointment.

The next morning, on May 11, 1999—a date I'll never forget—I walked into that doctor's office and was greeted by a woman at the front desk.

She spoke no English, and I still spoke no Portuguese, but I tried to say I was there to see Dr. Alejandro. The clinic was packed, and she was extremely busy, gesturing for me to have a seat and wait for my turn, annoyed but polite. In that moment, I was tapped by the universe, drawn in by the receptionist's competence and put-together manner. *Now here's someone who has her act together and knows where she's going in life.* I had a seat as she requested, already feeling in my heart that I was destined to be with that confident, pissed-off woman and would eventually marry her.

Now, as you may have noticed, I'd never even had a girlfriend before that day. People around me had dated, married, and had families as I'd grown up, but I'd always been focused on school and my career, knowing I had no means of supporting a wife or children. I knew in my heart, however, that one day I would meet someone somewhere and, in that moment, know she would be my wife.

There was an old love song in India from a movie called *Sharabi* that talked about meeting a woman who would make the singer her own. Singer Mohammad Rafi sang:

"Kabhi na kabhi kahin na kahin koi na koi to aayega kabhi na kabhi kahin na kahin koi na koi to aayega apna mujhe banaayega dil mein mujhe basaayega kabhi na kabhi kahin na kahin koi na koi tho aayega"

Sometime, somewhere, someone will surely come

Sometime, somewhere, someone will surely come
Someone will make me their own
Will fill me in their heart
Sometime, somewhere, someone will surely come

I'd sing it to my mother, and she would laugh, delighted by my hope-less romanticism at such an early age. But I knew the day would come, perhaps at an airport or in the library at school. Finally, the moment had arrived at a doctor's office in Campinas, Brazil.

Of course, you can't just walk up to an irritated woman and insist she's your soulmate while she's working. I said nothing to her and, after waiting my turn, saw Dr. Alejandro about my knees. Thankfully, it turned out that I had just stressed my muscles and ligaments by running on the sand and no serious damage had been done.

On my way out, I stopped at the counter and wrote on a piece of paper in English: *Hi, my name is Ravi. I'd like to speak with you. Here's my phone number.* She took a look at my tattered note but had no idea what it said. I left the situation as it was, said goodbye, and headed home. Later, she got someone at the clinic to translate my English so she could give me a call. Her name was Lilian.

We met that evening after work at my hotel. I had nothing in my room to offer aside from fruit, so I gave her a banana. She laughed at how odd I was, but I had never made an effort to be anyone but myself. After talking that night, we met a few more times.

Soon, her parents came into town, and I happened to meet them one day, along with her sister, who she lived with. Again, we couldn't communicate well, but we tried the best we could to make sense of each other. Then, her parents invited me to their place for the weekend, forty-five minutes away. Lilian was embarrassed, considering we'd essentially just met and didn't want me to go (which I didn't hear about until much later) but I accepted right away. We sat and talked the whole night on the floor of their living room. While the women were looking away, I looked at her father and gestured the act of putting a ring on my finger. He got the message, understanding I meant business. By the time I left, he and Lilian's mom and sister had a feeling I was the right man for her.

Lilian, however, was not yet convinced. I came from a culture with a tradition of arranged marriage where it was common for people to marry without knowing each other well, but that wasn't the case for her. She needed more time.

I gladly put in that time, of course, meeting all the members of her family who lived in the area. On weekends, we would meet and drive to Sao Paulo, where most of Lilian's relatives lived.

In India, we say that when you marry someone; you marry their family too.

With that perspective in mind, I wanted to meet them all and see what they were like. I was never shy about sitting in the middle of the family as everyone talked, trying to make jokes. They all seemed to like me aside from one of her uncles, who was rightfully worried I might be a con artist of some sort. Imagine meeting a guy from India who says he went to graduate school in the US, works for a German company, travels the world for work, and can't say exactly when he'll be able to return to Brazil again. It was a fair concern, and I accepted his scrutiny.

In the meantime, my parents were in the middle of moving to a new house in India, and I hadn't been able to get in touch with them. My dad had just retired and bought a new apartment. I left a message with one of my sisters, and finally one day, my phone rang at work. It was my dad, and I told him I'd been trying to reach him. I asked whether everything was okay. He said yes, and then asked me a strange question in a tone I'd never heard from him before.

"Ravi," he said, "are you all set?"

"What do you mean, Dad?"

But it was clear to me what he'd meant by that. He'd had a feeling I'd finally found my person. I laughed, understanding.

"Yes, Dad. I'm set."

Ravi posing on the rock in March 1999

Ravi getting engaged on the same rock as above, August 1999

After enough time had passed, Lilian and I built trust between one another and knew at some point we would marry. It was simply a matter of when and how. My plan was to take her to India and introduce her to my family, eventually. However, the plans for my project at work were cut short, and we had to sort our situation out quickly. We got engaged on August 28, a few months after we met, standing on a big rock on the first beach I'd ever been to in Brazil with the waves crashing around us. It's strange how the universe works. In March 1999 during a team visit to that beach, I had stood on that very rock with a friend. I told him that whenever I got married and whoever it was to, I would probably do it there. It felt like an omen. Six months later, that's where I proposed.

Lilian and I then had to get through the paperwork to travel to India and the US, something nearly impossible at the time, but we knew we'd make it work. We finally got married at a court in Brazil on October 2. The day of the ceremony, my father-in-law asked, "Are you sure you want to marry her?"

Ravi and Lillian's wedding, October 1999 in Brazil

I laughed, but he was serious, giving me one last chance to back out before we made things official, in case I wasn't truly committed.

"Look," he said, "she's not easy to deal with. Especially in the morning, she's not in a good mood."

I didn't quite catch everything he was telling me in Portuguese, and I knew things between Lilian and I would never be perfect, but I simply said yes. I was sure. I had an element of faith. When I saw her family and the way they lived, I understood their ways and felt they aligned well with my values. That, along with how I felt about her, was good enough for me. I had no doubts. It just felt right. This reminded me of what my dad would always say when I was young—that marriage is a blessing for some, a disguise for others, and a risk for all.

"Your heart knows the way. Run in that direction."

—Rumi, poet, theologian, and scholar

By then, I had learned to be decisive, even with an absence of information. I had come to understand that all decisions must flow from the heart to the brain, not the other way around. My understanding of who I was led me to see how I might complement others and what I brought to the table before asking anyone for partnership, be it with a life partner, friend, or coworker. No one is perfect, myself included. Whoever I decided to partner with in any endeavor would be imperfect as well. It would require sincere and sustained effort to create the masterpiece of our lives. But I was ready to listen to the signals sent to me by my heart. I was fully present, engaged in the moment, following the path the universe was laying out for me with clarity on how to proceed.

After the wedding, Lilian and I finished the process of getting her a spousal visa for the US. From the get-go, she knew I was based in Miami and that marrying me would mean leaving everything she had ever known behind in Brazil, including her family. While she had a few doubts about this, she had always been interested in traveling and learning English, which were both main features of my lifestyle at the time. She also loved me, clearly, though I can't speak for her about why. Maybe it was because she knew I'd been serious about her from the moment I saw her. Maybe it was my drive, ambition, or sense of excitement about things most people considered mundane. Maybe it was my cooking or my adventurous nature. Maybe it was because I wanted a family like she did. All I know is that I was thrilled she gave me a chance.

From Brazil, we set out for India where we would marry again, this time with my family present. The tickets were expensive, and we had to get a loan to cover them in the end. Lilian's father couldn't join us, unfortunately, but her mother came along for the trip. Door to door, we traveled for sixty hours. Part of me was nervous because, although I'd traveled around the world, Lilian had never left Brazil.

"What's India like?" she asked before we left.

"Expect the unexpected," I told her.

University of Life

LESSON #8: BEING DECISIVE AND PRESENT

Many believe the present moment holds unparalleled opportunities, and the power of decision making is unmatched. Decision shapes destiny. By moving forward confidently, staying present, and acting decisively, we have the potential to transform our lives as we desire. Can you recall a decision that transformed your life?

NINE

Adventures as a Couple

"It's a funny thing, coming home. Nothing changes. Every-
thing looks the same, feels the same, even smells the same.
You realize what's changed is you."

—Eric Roth, American screenwriter

It had been many years since I'd last seen India. My parents had recently moved into a brand-new apartment complex that wasn't ready to be lived in yet. The construction was finished, but the rooms hadn't been cleaned. Before Lilian, her mother, and I arrived, my father had asked the fifteen other tenants who were set to move into the building if they would delay their arrival until after my wedding so our friends and family could stay there. Thankfully, they were friends of my father already and all agreed, giving us their blessing.

I was dead tired when we got there, but more concerned about Lilian and her mom. They didn't speak the language, know anything about the local food, or realize just how crowded the place would be. It was a shock to see people all over the place from the moment we landed. Strangers would talk to them and afford them less personal space than they were used to. All around them were situations that could be misconstrued if one didn't know how to handle them. I had to keep my eyes and ears open in order to make sure they felt safe and comfortable.

We arrived at my father's apartment and were greeted by nearly 300 people, from close friends to immediate family to distant relatives. I realized right away that though the building was nice, it wasn't suitable to stay in yet. I dragged a group of people with me to the market to buy cleaning supplies so I could scrub splotches of paint off the floor. Over the next twenty-four hours, we divided the work and cleaned every single room to prepare for the arrival of more guests. It was touching to see family and friends who had come from far-off places to attend the wedding as a mark of respect, love, and affection for me and my family. Many had not seen me since my birth or very early in my childhood. Their presence was a blessing for the life I was about to embark on with Lilian.

We hadn't done much planning for the wedding. We simply showed up, got married on the terrace of my parents' apartment complex, and celebrated afterward with everyone there. During the rest of the trip, I realized my spontaneous, head-first way of diving into situations doesn't work for everyone.

I've always been fine with diving right into new situations, fully immersing myself—a bit like shock therapy for sparking significant change.

Lilian and her mom found this challenging though. They spoke no English, my family spoke no Portuguese, and yours truly still only knew a few words of Portuguese at the time. Every conversation between us involved gestures, drawings, dictionaries, and writing, but none of us could ever be quite sure we were being fully understood. To top this all off, the wedding itself had been overwhelming for them. It had been crowded there, as it was everywhere in India, because weddings in my country involve the entire extended family. We have rituals that can seem nonsensical to non-natives, and being told what to wear or eat can feel too forceful. In the end, Lilian and her mom understood the love and care that lay behind each request, even without a common language for everyone to connect through. After that experience, I understood the importance of making conscientious plans so my new wife would have the information she needed before our travels together.

We returned from India to Brazil to drop off my mother-in-law before flying to Miami. The language barrier was still causing significant challenges for us. When we got to Florida, I wanted to take Lilian to my favorite Thai restaurant. I had gone there several times in the past and always had a good experience. However, on this special day, as Lilian was looking forward to having her first lunch in the USA, every single dish smelled like fish, which she couldn't eat. Lilian, a long-time vegetarian, was in tears at this development. I didn't have the words to explain to her what had happened as I had never experienced the taste of fish in any dish I had eaten there as a vegetarian myself. It was a huge surprise.

Slowly but steadily, Lilian began to learn English on her own.

I would come home from work and see page after page of written English as part of Lilian's self-study journey. I also made an effort to speak conversational Portuguese to communicate with her. It was a slow process, and we knew it would take time.

A few months later, we combined our honeymoon and a business trip into one adventure, heading to London for about two weeks. I had planned to open an eloborate coworking, workout, and relaxation place at Heathrow Airport, because at the time nothing like it existed anywhere in the world. It was cold there as we walked through the city, viewing sites like the Tower Bridge. She didn't seem to want to go to the top of it with me. I told her to wait for me at the bottom, but she didn't understand what I had said. When I got back down, she was gone, off looking for me somewhere.

After a while, we found each other, and she was clearly upset by the miscommunication. Not a great start to our romantic trip.

In our own broken way, we sorted things out and headed to the subway station next. When our train arrived, I jumped inside, but she somehow wasn't able to board before the doors closed. The train left, and I saw her on the platform through the window, gesturing for her to meet me at the next stop. Thankfully, she understood and made it, but again, she was pissed. Strike two.

Finally, we made it back to our hotel in one piece. We didn't have much money to go out to eat, so we bought a bunch of food to keep in the room with us. Unfortunately, though the place was beautiful, our room didn't have a fridge. There was a ledge outside the window, however, and we would leave our food there all night to keep it chilled, making do with what we had. Lilian and I managed for nearly two weeks there and ended up having a wonderful time despite our occasional ups and downs and miscommunications. There was a sense of joy between us, and we were enthralled to see London for the first time together.

Back when I was preparing for our trip to India before our second wedding, I researched Heathrow Airport online, as we would be transferring flights there. At the time, I learned that 69 million people went through Heathrow annually and the average wait for international fliers was four hours. That number stuck in my head, and I smelled a business opportunity. I began to collect data and connect remotely with key folks all over the UK to make a business plan for a one-of-a-kind center for relaxation and coworking spaces at airports. Such centers exist in terminals all over the world today, but they didn't back in 1999. Much of the concept was based on my own experience as a frequent flier. I imagined a place where travelers would be able to shower and get a massage; a place to play with their kids, stocked with diapers and baby food. There would be a concierge service that brought them meals or anything else available in the terminal. Movies, books, beds for naps, you name it! I was sure the idea would be a hit.

I met with countless people in London during my honeymoon, from architects to bankers to the regional head of Sony, who all gave me great advice. Lilian didn't mind and was excited for me, knowing I had a good idea to pitch. Some of the people I spoke to told me that the British Airport Authority (BAA) was very brand conscious, and since I was a nobody, it would be helpful to partner with someone in the four biggest consulting companies, who all had solid contacts with British authority members. I eventually made contact with one of them and scheduled a visit with him and his team. Everyone was friendly but dropped a bombshell on me: I would need to pay 10,000 British pounds for them to accompany me to present the business plan to potential partners, irrespective of the outcome.

"I may be a consultant," I told them, "But I'm not a fool. Why would I give you that money with no guarantee of success?"

Normally, I'm not a man who lets fear stand in his way.

If I had been single at the time, I might have raised the money, invested, and gone through with the deal. However, Lilian's family was already nervous about my huge amount of debt. In Brazil, it was unheard of to have taken $100,000 in personal loans, and though I'd always been transparent about my situation, it was impossible to diffuse their worries. My gut was telling me to move forward with the offer, but with the language barrier at play between me and Lilian's family, it was not easy to express my feelings to them. Taking on more debt would worry them.

We returned to Miami from London. There, I let my fear take over and gave up on my idea after twelve months of working to make it happen. To my surprise and disappointment years later, business centers and coworking spaces became a reality at airports around the world. I don't regret the decision I made at the time, but the memory still pops up, and I wonder what would have happened if I'd taken out another loan and followed through.

In the least, I learned to take more time to question my fears in order to avoid missed opportunities.

That little boy back in Sindri who dusted himself off and got back on his dad's scooter to take another round hadn't succumbed to his fears, and I wasn't about to let him down.

*"Think, act, and talk with enthusiasm
and you will attract positive results."*

—Micheal LeBoeuf, author

Back in Miami, my company told me about a project in Colombia that was having major problems. Our team had moved on from the assignment months before, but my boss wanted someone to go help our client with their difficulties. I was offered the chance to go, thanks to my reputation for getting things done with a no-nonsense approach. Back in 2000, Colombia was rife with danger, and few people were willing to work there. At home, I discussed the opportunity with Lilian, and we made a decision to accept the assignment and were given three days to prepare before departing.

Despite my acceptance of the assignment, I only had theoretical familiarity with the subject matter: dunning and collections. If you don't pay your phone bill, depending on how the software was configured, the company can suspend your account and send you a letter or two. If payment still isn't made, a collection agency might be called to get in touch with you. In Colombia, tons of my client's customers suddenly started getting letters in the mail falsely stating their bills had not been paid. This had created a huge PR disaster that I was tasked with investigating and cleaning up as soon as possible. Whether or not I succeeded could make or break my career. After my experience in London, though, I was wary of passing up opportunities. So, with little notice, we packed our bags and flew to Bogota.

In preparation for the visit, I reached out to a select group of subject-matter experts in my company, including the developers who had created the solution I'd be utilizing. They had implemented our company's telecom solution, including the dunning and collections functionality for our client, but had wrapped up the project and left months earlier, due to Colombia's dire security situation at the time. Over the phone and through email, those colleagues and I went over all kinds of scenarios that I might encounter in Colombia and how to resolve them. I also got their consent to seek support from them after I got there.

In the early 2000s, ongoing guerrilla warfare involving several armed groups was ravaging Colombia, creating a complex and terrifying situation for everyone in the country. The two primary guerrilla groups, the Revolutionary Armed Forces of Colombia (FARC) and the National Liberation Army (ELN), were in direct conflict with the government. Civilians often found themselves caught in the crossfire, leading to displacement, human rights abuses, and a desperate humanitarian crisis. Because of all this, my company had hired a driver named Carlos to pick Lilian and me up at the airport and be our guide throughout the trip. We could only go to places he was allowed to take us to.

After dropping my wife off at the hotel, Carlos brought me to my client's office, and I met with the CEO and COO of the company, as well as other members of their team. The CEO began by informing me that the reputation was being harmed by the product my company had developed and implemented. No pressure at all for a guy who just landed! I asked them to tell me everything that had happened. I was armed with questions I had prepared so I could suss out the issue at hand. They answered my questions, and I asked if they'd be available to assist me in my investigation during my time there. They all agreed to offer whatever help they could, and in that fashion, I formed a great support team.

While I was being briefed, a loud explosion met our ears, it sounded like a bomb had gone off in the distance. Within seconds, everyone but me was in tears.

The COO then explained to me that everyone there had lost someone to local violence, whether they had been murdered or kidnapped by the guerillas. I asked if we could take a break to allow everyone time to gather themselves, and they all left the room, aside from the COO.

I leveled with the guy, telling him I had experience and had done a lot of research in preparation for this assignment but wasn't an expert on the problems they were experiencing. I would need time to analyze their database and come up with targeted recommendations. He agreed to my plan and from there, I went to work.

I got back to the hotel late, meaning Lilian had been alone all day. The next two weeks were much the same, with me practically living at my client's office, which was tough on her. With the help of both my local and Miami teams, we sorted the issue out successfully. It turned out their new database hadn't been configured correctly, creating a number of issues. I managed to sort things out in a way that satisfied both the client and my company and boosted my confidence in my leadership skills in the process.

On weekends, Lilian and I would visit areas of the city that were deemed safe, working to avoid dangerous hotspots. Our driver Carlos had been intimately impacted by the fighting going on around us, like most everyone we met during our trip, having lost his brother and sister in a bombing. There were kind, good-hearted people all over Colombia, but every one of them had inner scars.

Lilian and I had a wonderful time in Bogotá! We savored amazing Italian food, visited a top-rated café in a repurposed prison turned national museum, explored the stunning Museum of Gold, and were awed by the Catedral de Sal de Zipaquirá, a church built over 600 feet underground in a salt mine.

This trip was pivotal, bringing us closer and enhancing our communication and understanding. Yet, it was challenging for Lilian at times since my work kept me busy, but it was a memorable experience for both of us.

It was a short assignment, only lasting two months, but the experience was deeply impactful. Not only had I solved the problem, but my results also boosted my reputation, making it clear I was someone who could solve important challenges. Helping our client through that crisis was a huge win for our company. Carlos also left an imprint on my heart as someone who was willing to put himself in danger on our behalf in spite of all he'd been through. He had served as yet another example of people in this world who live without title, fame, or fortune. They show up and do their job so others can do theirs. They are the everyday, unassuming, unrecognized heroes that keep society going.

Lilian gave birth to our first daughter in 2001, which was a time of great maturation for us. As many parents will attest, it's hard to describe the feeling of holding your baby for the first time. It changes you, your values, and your priorities. I had always thought I would become a father someday but hadn't expected how much joy my kid would bring into my life.

We didn't want to know the sex of the baby before she was born and had come up with three male and three female names as options. We shared them with our extended families in India and Brazil and asked for their input. We wanted a name that would be easy to pronounce for speakers from all over the world but also one that stood for something meaningful.

When my daughter arrived, we named her Sasha, as it garnered the most votes among our little committee. It means "defender" and "helper of mankind" in Hindi.

Cake to celebrate Sasha's birth, 2001

Over the moon after Sasha's birth, I ordered a huge custom cake that had to be transported to my office in Miami in a mini-truck, where about 300 colleagues joined my wife and me in celebration. The cake was designed to represent our child's combined heritage: the union of three cultures— the USA, India, and Brazil.

But along with this period of joy and celebration came the swift realization that my wife's attitude toward motherhood was rapidly changing. She had prepared so many things for Sasha's arrival, but soon after the birth, none of it seemed to matter to her anymore. She had lost energy, patience, and interest in being a mother, all in very short order. We would soon discover these feelings were symptomatic of a classic case of postpartum depression. I wasn't sure what to do for Lilian and worried about her headspace while I was busy at the office.

Barely two weeks into this crisis at home, 9/11 happened. Who among us could possibly forget where we were on that day? I was driving to work when I heard on the radio that two planes had hit the World Trade Center. Upon entering my office, I saw the meeting I was scheduled to attend had been canceled, and my colleagues and I watched the day unfold on TV, along with the rest of the country. Some people there made emotional, discriminatory comments against Muslims and immigrants, knowing full well we had people working there from all over the world.

Rumors about what was happening spread like wildfire, and Lilian called me after seeing the news, asking me to come home as soon as possible. She was afraid of what might happen to immigrants whose skin looked like mine. I called friends around the country to tell them to be careful and protect their kids from the deranged extremists coming out of the woodwork.

In the days after, a Sikh man in Texas was attacked while wearing a turban out in public. A brown-skinned friend of mine was held at the airport in Boston for questioning due to his skin color. This all reminded me of the atmosphere in New Delhi following Indira Gandhi's assassination when I was eighteen. Distrust was the name of the game. Citizens turned on one another left and right out of fear and prejudice.

I repeated to others what Mahatma Gandhi had said when hooligans in South Africa threatened to pelt him with rocks: "You will find there's room for us all."

I feared what the future might hold for my new baby and how the heated rhetoric against immigrants could impact how the world treated her.

Lilian, Sasha, and I were supposed to fly to Brazil for a new project, but the trip was delayed while things were calming down. Finally, we were permitted to fly when air travel was deemed safe again and arrived in late September 2001 with a heavy, somber cloud hanging over our heads. I had no assurances of how long my job would last, due to whispers of instability arising at my company. I felt drained of energy regularly, rarely getting more than four hours of sleep per night, struggling to take care of my vulnerable new family. Most days, I had to fight hard not to doze off during meetings.

I kept running though. On the treadmill at my hotel gym, I'd have Sasha next to me in her bassinet so Lilian could rest. My tiny daughter, full of boundless energy, kept me on my toes, shaking me awake, jolting me back to attention. There were new stakes now, far higher than before, and protecting what I had built would take everything I had within me.

Yet, in an odd way, I found myself fully energized about life as a newly minted dad and a family man. I was no longer the boy who dreamed of nothing more than playing cricket for India. My mind was brimming with wonderful ideas and dreams for the future of my young family, and I retained a youthful spirit in my heart when it came to my thoughts and outlook.

University of Life

LESSON #9: THE DANCE OF FEAR

Our fear often stems from a lack of information. It is a formidable dance partner rather than something to avoid. Drawing on our life experiences, we can overcome fear by committing to our decisions, owning our outcomes, and moving forward. When have you overcome fear in the past?

TEN

Corporate Showdowns

"Sometimes you meet yourself back where you started, but stronger."

—Yrsa Daley-Ward, English writer, model, and actor

All things considered, my career had been going fairly well prior to my assignment in Brazil at the end of 2001. I had already taken on several leadership opportunities after my success in Colombia. At some point, however, the German company I worked for was bought by a multinational oil engineering conglomerate, which didn't make sense to anyone on my team. Why would an oil exploration company buy a company focused on telecommunications?

Some of our new executives came to Miami soon after to explain their story to us, which was that everything would continue to be business as usual. None of us were buying it. I had spent the last four plus years of my career there and wasn't about to let a bunch of corporate bigwigs take advantage of the amazing colleagues I'd formed relationships with. Ever a rebel like my grandparents and in the interest of transparency, I raised my hand.

"Stop treating us like kids," I told them. "When are you closing this office?"

They tried to assure us nothing of the sort would happen. That we'd be able to keep our jobs. Regardless, tension grew among my colleagues and myself. We all worried about what would happen to our legal status if they laid us off, as the majority of us were immigrants on employment visas of some sort. If we lost our jobs while we happened to be working on a project abroad, would we be able to reenter the US, particularly in the context of such a hostile political environment?

Would we be able to get back to our families and sort out our living situations or end up stranded in a foreign land?

It was amid this rising anxiety that my family and I traveled to Brazil from Miami on a project assignment. Soon after, the company sent its executives there to appease employees, this time taking us all out to dinner. The head of the North American division, a man named John, showed up at our office in Belo Horizonte alongside a group of executives. They pretended to be concerned about our welfare, but the underlying feelings of mistrust and anger towards them were palpable. According to what we'd ascertained from a few emails that had passed around the office, the company was already working on halting green-card processing for immigrants on work visas despite the fact that those processing fees had already been paid for.

One of my Belgian colleagues, fed up and a bit drunk, finally snapped and called them out. "You're all LIARS! We know you're going to close our office."

He then looked to John and asked him when we would lose our jobs. John didn't answer, again sidestepping the questions and performing the song and dance he was so adept at. I had read about corporate politics and the lack of integrity displayed by so-called "leaders." Now, there I was, witnessing it firsthand in real time. It was disappointing beyond belief but not surprising. I felt an urge to lay out conflicting emails we had all gathered but knew that dinner wasn't the time or place to bring up the topic of our green cards.

Impatient and disgusted by the mixed messages we were getting, I decided to fly to Atlanta on my own dime after John had returned to the head office so I could confront him on the matter there once and for all. Those in charge were already closing that regional office, laying its people off, and we were almost certainly next on the chopping block. I wanted to ensure that if the Latin American division in Miami was to meet the same fate, we could at least come out on the other side as well off as possible.

C-suite fat cats have a penchant for upending the lives of their workforce without notice and disappearing into the ether without so much as a shrug or apology, dodging legal protections for workers on their way out.

I wasn't about to let that happen to us. If they were about to discard us, I would make them do it legally. I told Lilian my plan, saying I might not have a job when I returned to Brazil, but that I needed to try my hardest to do the right thing for the team, even if it meant sticking my neck out.

They say that in tough times, people's true colors come through. During that unstable period, I witnessed several acts of disloyalty among colleagues attempting to jockey for favor in order to salvage their jobs. Some left our project at the halfway point, abandoning ship prematurely in an attempt to hop to other positions within the company. I would have loved to keep my position as well, of course, but not if it would mean working for leaders who lacked empathy. The executive team had not taken my team's concerns seriously in Brazil. If I had to become a thorn in their side in order to be heard, so be it.

I flew to Atlanta and drove straight to the office of the head of the North American division, unbeknownst to anyone who worked with me, not wanting to bother the team with my choice. I didn't have an appointment, and John's assistant tried to stop me, but I barged in regardless, knowing I had come bearing credible evidence, and asked whether he remembered me. He said no.

"I'm one of the guys you came to talk to in Brazil last week. One of the guys you said you won't be laying off."

That seemed to jog his memory, but I could smell his insincerity. Callousness and fear simmered behind the mask.

"I'm not leaving here," I told him, "Until you do something about what's happening with all employees on nonimmigrant visas."

"And what's that?"

"You just bought this company," I said. "A company my colleagues and I have helped build for years. That was a business transaction, and you'll do whatever you feel you need to do financially. All I'm asking is that you act with a sense of integrity and fairness."

I told him the vast majority of the folks in Miami he was about to lay off were on work visas and waiting for their green cards to be processed, on the brink of achieving permanent residency.

"From what I understand, you're halting those processes, which have already been paid for. If you go through with that, you have no idea of the destruction you'll cause. These people have missed time with their families and missed important events to build your company—the one you're about to milk for profit."

John kept trying to play games with me, dismissing my concerns and questioning whether I knew what I was talking about. I told him he saw his employees as numbers, but I saw them as friends.

"You really know them?" he asked.

"Yes."

The next thing I knew, he turned around and picked up a pile of papers from his printer. It had the names of the employees of the Miami team, and he began quizzing me on them one by one. I knew everyone he mentioned, along with their husbands, wives, and kids, and was able to speak in detail about them.

John still looked down on me with arrogance, even after I'd passed his little test. I countered with a test of my own, showing him the thick folder, I'd brought with printed copies of the email chains filled with the contradictory messages we'd received since his company had bought us out. I told him point blank that I wanted his guarantee in writing that he wouldn't stop any processes related to our green cards or residency.

"If you can't give me that guarantee in writing," I said, "I'll go straight to the US immigration office and let them know you're stranding people—who are all here *legally*—outside the country on assignments and sending mixed messages about the situation. They were hired in the USA, and you can't fire them while they're abroad. You'll be in a legal bind if you do."

John, now up to speed and nervous about how serious I was, picked up the phone and called the global head of HR. She spoke to me over the phone, trying to tell me she'd take care of the matter, but I stuck to my guns and refused to leave until I had that guarantee in writing. Finally, they capitulated and gave me what I asked for. I turned to leave and as I walked out the door, John called out to me, offering to pay for my travel expenses.

"I don't take charity," I told him, and left in disgust. I had been helped by a lot of people in my life, but I could never accept it from people who lacked so much integrity.

To this day, every colleague I advocated for is still in the US legally. They're still productive citizens, and their kids are doing well. Eventually, many people were indeed laid off as anticipated. I was allowed to keep my job a bit longer but asked to move back to the Atlanta office. Two days after arriving there, I lost my job too.

The whole experience had amounted to a loss of innocence for me and my colleagues. We were hardworking people who cared about our clients, careers, and each other. We had poured our hearts and souls into that company, only to be thrown into a desperate situation by people like John who cared more about their bottom line than the lives of good people.

I've worked for enough companies and led enough teams by now to know that showing true integrity takes courage, but costs very little. With a human touch, those executives could have done exactly what I demanded without being asked. They could have taken the responsibility to treat their workforce like human beings rather than objects to be discarded.

To see that level of callousness weighed heavily on my heart, but the lesson my colleagues and I learned was an important one: Companies exist to make a profit and everything else is secondary. The earlier people can understand this during their careers, the better.

You can land a dream job with a high salary and fancy title, but that's no guarantee of stability in the long run. We can all end up feeling like we're moving backwards, struggling again in ways we thought we'd moved on from, and we can't let this stop or defeat us.

After getting laid off in 2002 in Atlanta, I left Lilian and Sasha at my in-laws' house in Brazil and returned to Miami to move our stuff back to Atlanta. We were trying to save on expenses while I was out of a job. Luckily, I had a cousin in town who was kind enough to let me stay at her place for six months. It was hard on my family and me to be away from each other. I missed playing with Sasha and worried about Lilian's health.

In July of that year, they were able to join me back in Atlanta, along with my mother-in-law. She was a huge help in taking care of Sasha, which allowed me to work my butt off to pass different certification exams in Atlanta so I could stay competitive in the marketplace.

My interest in relational databases hadn't diminished since I'd taken a class on it in Charlotte several years before. I decided to get certified as an Oracle database administrator. Those courses were not cheap, upwards of $5,000 on average. I looked around Atlanta for the right course and eventually called an instructor who taught at a local technical college. I wanted to know a bit about his teaching style and approach.

"You want to learn something? You come to my class. If you don't want to learn, sit at home. Up to you."

His directness felt harsh at first, but I valued the sincerity in his straightforward approach and paid the five grand to enroll. It was a big deal for me financially, but the teacher was knowledgeable, energetic, and seemed trustworthy. An immigrant from Mozambique, he had been through many trials similar to my own and kept it real while talking about the ways of the world.

While taking the course, I was offered work in a different area of Atlanta at a global IT company, which I desperately needed. I would still wake up at around 4:00 in the morning, do an intense workout in the apartment complex's gym, take care of Sasha in the morning, go to work, then sit in Atlanta's notorious evening traffic to get to the Oracle class, which went from 6:00 to 9:00 p.m. Then I'd do self-study until midnight.

My new job was very stressful for the eighteen months I stayed there.

The men in charge were good, smart guys for the most part but entirely focused on money. It seemed to me some of them didn't even care about their own families enough to return their calls during the day.

One time, we had a major company initiative to find out why we were losing money on certain contracts we had with various airlines around the world. The CFO and my boss told me they wanted me to figure out exactly how much money was being lost so we could strategize on how to recover all or some of the lost revenue. I took on the challenge, and it took me a month to perform my analysis. As I was preparing to present it to the CFO, I was steamrolled by my boss, who asked another member of my team to present the information I had prepared. My only guess for why he did this was that he felt the need to knock me down a peg in order to prove his status.

I didn't want to make drama in front of the CFO. He himself inquired as to why I was not presenting the findings and recommendations when I was the one who had worked on them. I made light of the situation, stating my colleague had better English and superior presentation skills. Truth be told, I was fuming inside at the complete lack of honor on the part of my boss and my colleague. As we were on the elevator coming down from the twenty-first floor after the meeting, I looked at both of them and told them they had no integrity whatsoever and I had lost respect for them.

They didn't say much in response, but the whole thing bothered me so much that I couldn't sleep that night. At 3:00 a.m., I went to the apartment's gym and ran for three hours, and as I did, I had an out-of-this-world experience, like someone was asking me questions and I was answering. Maybe it was me connecting deeply with my soul. Each progressive question led to additional clarity, and I came out of the gym knowing I would resign that coming Monday.

I got home that morning at six and told Lilian I needed to talk with her.

"I need to talk to you too," she said.

"Okay," I said. "Why don't you go first?

"I think you should quit your job."

My wife has always been keenly perceptive from the day I met her. She had seen how tired and stressed I'd become while working at that place. She knew I'd get sick if I kept going and wanted what was best for us and our daughter. I did too.

> *"Let yourself be drawn by the stronger pull of that which you truly love."*
>
> —Rumi, poet, theologian, and scholar

We were so happy to discover how in sync we were that we got dressed up and went out to celebrate our decision. On the way, we took a wrong turn and accidentally ended up at a BMW dealership.

"What the heck," I told Lilian. "Let's go and take a test drive."

Seeing how we were dressed, the car salespeople there came running to ask what we were looking for. I'd never driven a BMW and told them I wanted something from their M Series. The feeling of being behind the wheel was fantastic, and for the first time in a long time, I felt completely free and playful, which cemented my earlier decision to quit my job.

The next time you want to make a major decision, go take a test drive in a BMW. It just might change your life!

When Lilian and I got back from our celebration, I wrote my resignation letter. Monday morning, I walked into my boss's room and gave it to him.

"So, what are you planning to do next, Ravi?" he asked, not particularly surprised by my decision.

"All I know for certain is that I don't want to work here with you. I'll figure out what to do next, but I'll never work another day at this job."

The look on my boss's face was worth capturing. He'd went to one of the top engineering institutions in the US. Here was a man who was smart and capable but chasing titles and status. He couldn't imagine someone resigning from a well-paying, prestigious job over someone else's lack of integrity. I didn't take his behavior personally then and still don't, but I'm not sure he ever realized how harmful his actions were and how poorly they reflected on who he was.

If there's one thing I've learned after all these years, it's that "people skills" are nonnegotiable in a leader. Men like him have provided me with ample clarity about what not to do and who not to be.

I had saved up a bit of money by then, and for the first time since I'd left India in 1988, I decided to take six months off to reconnect with myself and do some deep reflection. Lilian took Sasha to Brazil to visit her family while I spent a month in Tilakpur, my ancestral village where I'd spent every summer until twelfth grade. My parents had recently retired there, and I spent my days walking along the banks of the Ganges, talking with some of the young kids in the area. Many had nothing on them but the clothes they were wearing but were happy-go-lucky all the same. I filed their carefree expressions away in my memory bank to be accessed on demand when I needed to feel grounded. Life can still be full of vitality and joy in the absence of creature comforts.

Ravi's village, dry river bed

From India, I ended up going to London to spend some time with my youngest sister, Archana, who was working there as a holistic fitness coach. I then went to France and spent some time in Paris before heading to Brazil to meet up with Lilian's side of the family. Finally, the three of us returned to Atlanta, where I ended up getting hired at one of the biggest software companies in the telecommunications space. They were expanding at lightning speed and even employed a couple of my friends from the German company that had laid us all off.

It was 2005, and my new job was going well, sending me around the country to different locations. The year before, I had paid off all my student loans, which was a huge milestone in my life. I had managed to do this by saving the daily extended travel bonus of $35 plus the per diem provided by my company per the US State Department guide-lines. It was like a brick had been sitting on my head and was suddenly knocked off, relieving me of a tremen-dous weight. In my mind, it had never been a question of whether I'd pay off all my debts, but when.

Ravi's village, at a farm with local kids

Ravi's village, dry river bed

Ravi with local kids at the mango orchard in the village

Soon after, Lilian and I saved enough to make a twenty percent down payment on our first house and moved in shortly after. We poured all our savings into our new place, and my parents finally made plans to visit us the following year. What had once been a distant dream of home owner-ship had finally come true.

Making plans to welcome my parents to our new home in the US marked a momentous occasion. It would be their first (and, to date, only) trip outside of India. In my mind, nothing I had achieved would have been possible without their love, guidance, and support. Their lifelong example of how to build a life one step at a time left a deep impression on me. I still vividly remember them paying for our first fridge, record player, and everything else for the house in cash. There were no loans or credit cards back then. We had all learned to save and survive together as a family, and I looked forward to showing them their impact on me.

I had requested four days of time off six months in advance of their arrival in Atlanta. But when I returned home a day before they flew in, I got an email from my project director saying that unless there was a death in my family, he expected me to come into work the following Monday. His message sent a chill through me, bringing all the harshness of corporate America back to my attention.

This lack of humanity wasn't an isolated incident at my company. I'd had a colleague, Raman, who I had worked with for eighteen months. One day, as a result of a delay, he'd been mercilessly chewed out by our project director in front of several people. I'd been furious on his behalf, aware of the quality of his character. Shortly thereafter, he resigned and went on to start his own company, which employs more than two thousand people globally today. Following his example, I put in my resignation, CCing every leader there to say I wouldn't wish such treatment on anyone. Being loyal to my family was nonnegotiable.

Since those days, I've somehow been able to block out all the noise of the world and build my personal ethos by keeping an open mind, staying focused on my target.

I've worked hard to maintain an inclusive approach and lead my life for myself and my family first, followed by those I worked with. While I think it's important to call out wrongdoing, it always was and still is critical to me not to become cynical about life. We have to be able to trust one another as human beings.

Corporations hold power, but so do we. Living, breathing human beings just like us hide behind their titles in order to oppress us. They share many of the same needs, feelings, and challenges we do and it's our task to find reason-rooted means of reaching them. It's our right to fight the wrongs of the world with all our might, even knowing we may not succeed.

University of Life

LESSON #10: UNLIMITED IDENTITY

All living beings possess multifaceted identities. We must steadfastly refuse to let anyone but ourselves define who we are, what we believe in, and what we stand for. This stance can come at a high cost but is always within our power. Never be anyone's doormat or allow them to decide who you are. What are some aspects of your multifaceted identity?

ELEVEN

Running for My Dream Job

"Hope is being able to see that there is light despite all of the darkness."

—Desmond Tutu, South African bishop and theologian

Not long after quitting my latest job in Atlanta, Lilian and I welcomed our second daughter, Sahara, into the world. We'd been so touched by the beauty of the desert during an assignment I took on in Egypt that we decided to bring the name into our family forever. I then found a new job with a small German company close to my house in May 2007. I was hired as a product manager, a position I'd never worked before. I signed up for a weekend certification course before my first day so I could learn how best to approach the new opportunity presented to me.

My first day of work was in San Diego, where my boss lived. I shook his hand and assessed his character after flying in from across the country. He was a fantastic fellow who'd hired four other people along with me. The company hadn't released a new product in three years and was losing market share. They were eager to set us loose and see what we could accomplish.

Ravi with his team on the boat in San Diego Bay, 2007

A few weeks later, my boss scheduled another meeting on a boat he had rented for us. I was set to give a presentation to my entire team, which I prepared by putting to use the knowledge I'd gained from the certification course and my years of experience delivering on projects globally. We all stayed for five days, meeting up to work in the mornings, then taking rides around the San Diego Bay, complete with an amazing chef. I loved the job, and things were seemingly going well.

In December of that year, the head of my company came to the US from Germany. My team had recently presented our proposal to the board on how to revamp our product management life cycle. Our work was well received, and we were able to release a new product, a software program for the utility billing industry, within six months. Our effort was paying off, and things were looking up for our group.

However, when the global CEO arrived, he laid off the CEO of the American division, all the product managers, and other people working regionally in one fell swoop.

Just like that, I lost my job while I had two very young kids, a wife, and a brand-new mortgage to support.

I was devastated once more, as my colleagues had been amazing, and the company had seemed like a place where I could blossom. At the very least, I already had my green card and, therefore, wouldn't have to deal with any threats to my residency status.

My family and I couldn't afford health insurance and decided to rely on the money we had in the bank. We had some saved but not enough, and we would soon be desperate. On top of all this, the 2007 recession was settling in, and unemployment was rampant all across America.

By fall of 2008, we were in dire straits, consuming only milk, cabbage, sweet potatoes, beans, bananas, berries, nuts, and the other basics necessary for proper nutrition, along with regular exercise. That was our health insurance plan.

I was working as hard as I could to find my next job. Everyone who knew me would ask me if I'd finally found one when we spoke. I never lost touch with the element of faith that I would find a way to make it work. Even in a tough job market, we would somehow survive. Many of the executives and job-seekers I spoke with in the job search meetings and support groups I attended had weak networks and lacked confidence in the future. People were shaken by the economic impact of the recession. They had all gotten their jobs based on connections in the past, but it seemed no one felt they could rely on anyone anymore.

I would encourage them by saying that though money was tight, we hadn't lost everything. We still had our families, our experience, and our education.

I would meet friends at coffee shops but bring water along with me. I'd find ways to see others without spending any money. In some places, even buying gas was hard because the price was too high to afford. Within six months, it became impossible to manage my family's financial situation. Lilian thought she might be able to work to help out, but it was impossible with two young kids at home. Eventually, we asked her sister to come up from Brazil and stay with us. She wanted to learn English, so I offered to enroll her in a free class and covered the cost of her plane ticket. She agreed and got a visa to stay for a few months.

Having Lilian's sister at home gave us some breathing room, and Lilian started working at a daycare center. It just about killed her to take care of multiple toddlers. She'd come home barely able to lift her arms due to exhaustion. She was making very little money, but it helped us buy food and other necessities.

By September, our ultimate fear came to pass. We had zero dollars in the bank. I felt like I was back at square one, broke all over again just as I had been in college.

I made it to thirty-six final job interviews that year but never got a single offer.

It was crushing, but I had no time to feel sorry for myself. I had a family to feed and a career to save.

It was during this challenging time that my seven-year-old daughter, Sasha, walked into my home office after I had just received yet another rejection. With her innocent curiosity, she asked, "Dad, what do they ask you in the meetings?" I shared a few things with her, and then, in a moment of profound introspection, she paused, looked up at me with her big, earnest eyes, and said, "Dad, just say enough." She wrapped her small arms around me in a heartfelt hug and then told me that she had asked all her teachers at elementary school to help me and that she would rake leaves to earn some money for the family. Her words and actions melted my heart and gave me the strength to keep going. Kids have an incredible innate sense about the human heart!

Back in early May of that year, I challenged all my fellow jobseekers to do something they had never done before then report back with their results during the following week's Monday meeting. I wanted to help break people's patterns with activities that could change everyone's mood and boost their confidence during our transition between jobs. They could read a new book, call someone they wanted to connect with, cook a brand-new dish, or something of that nature.

"It doesn't matter what your chosen activity is," I said, "but everyone must make a commitment to do something challenging."

Ravi and daughter Sahara at finish line

I declared that I would run twenty miles, a feat I'd never accomplished up to that point.

The most I had ever run was ten miles. Before the run, I had a T-shirt printed that said *JOGGING & WALKING FOR MY DREAM JOB*. As I ran, people would call out to me. I felt great upon reaching my goal and came home energized, full of ideas on what to do about our money problems.

I continued my job search with a new and renewed level of urgency, but when my family went broke that October, I knew I would need help. I called one of my friends from the University of Idaho, who had since moved to Atlanta. I also called another colleague from the German company I'd worked for previously. I told them about our financial situation and asked both for loans. They asked how much I needed. I said $10,000. They both wrote me checks for that amount, never asking when I'd be able to repay them. This helped me and my family cover our expenses for a bit.

At that point, having been rejected hundreds of times, and considering how my past colleagues and I had been treated, I was done with corporate culture. I made a firm decision to work for myself as an independent contractor rather than seeking permanent employment again. That's how I got my first break after a year and six days of unemployment.

I got a six-month contract at one of the world's largest conferencing companies, leading the implementation of their cloud-based solution in North America. I took the gig but was equally focused on pushing the next limit of my athletic pursuits. Running twenty miles for the first time in May was like a long meditation for me. One thought that had cemented itself at the end of the run was that if I could run twenty miles, I could definitely handle 26.2, the length of a full marathon. And from that moment, I became a marathon runner from the inside out. I transformed my thinking and my body responded accordingly, enabling me to push my limits.

Marathon training made it possible for me to be in a state of flow in spite of the realities I was faced with in life. It aligned in my body, mind, and soul.

For me, this simple act of doing something new for the first time opened up a world that I had never dreamed about and led to experiences I'm still grateful for. I'd caught the marathon bug and become addicted. In December 2008, I signed up for the Atlanta marathon, which was held in March 2009. I'd wake up every day at 2:30 a.m., run from three to six, come home, get ready, have breakfast, feed the kids, catch my bus to work, do my job, come home, go to the gym, lift weights, return home at 8:00 p.m., eat, read, and sleep for four hours before doing the whole thing again. I engaged in this endeavor for nine months while settling my bills and debts.

I completed my first marathon in five hours and forty minutes, feeling humbled and determined to improve in the future while also celebrating the year-long effort. Not only did I cross the finish line, but I also shattered my previous physical and mental limits and adopted new beliefs.

Right before my six-month contract came to an end, I told Lilian our situation was such that I'd be willing to travel anywhere for work, apart from Afghanistan and Iraq. There were telecom opportunities there, but I refused to put myself in the middle of those wars despite the money I could make. A week after my conversation with my wife, I

Ravi at the finish line with daughter, Sasha, 2009

got an email from a friend from the German company where I'd worked for five years. He had a month-long contract available for me immediately in Lima, Peru.

"When do you want me to come?" I asked.

"Now," he said. "Yesterday."

The timing was perfect. I went straight to the consulate to get the visa I would need. That same day, the results from my annual physical came back, showing that my cholesterol was high. I was perplexed by the result. There I was, running sixty miles a week and eating well. How was it possible? The doctor didn't try to investigate. Instead, he gave me a prescription for medicine I didn't want to take. I looked at him and told him he wasn't doing his job.

"Why do you say that?" he asked.

"You haven't asked me any questions about my lifestyle. Do I sleep enough? What's my diet like? Do I drink enough water? Wouldn't those factors have an effect on my results? You should be working with me to figure that out."

The man looked at me like I was crazy.

I left for Lima that night. When I arrived, I was so put off by my experience with the doctor in Atlanta that I went to my hotel room, took out a sheet of paper, and drew a line down the middle. What had changed in my life over the past six months? Nothing came to mind at first, but I finally realized what it was. I had started eating protein bars, which were essentially candy in terms of sugar content, though I hadn't known that at the time. I made a decision then and there to stop eating them cold turkey.

I had a kitchen in my hotel room and decided to start cooking without oil during my assignment there, which would also reduce my cholesterol. I joined a Pilates class across the street, too, and found a beautiful spot to run by the ocean. I ate fresh fruits and vegetables along with whole grains. Treating my symptoms rather than seeking the causes of my health issues would never satisfy me, so I knew I'd need to experiment to solve the mystery myself.

"Never underestimate your power to change yourself."

—H. Jackson Brown, Jr., American author

I started reading books about health and nutrition, which soon became an addiction. I began attending conferences and got to meet some of the pioneers of the plant-based nutrition field, including Dr. T. Colin Campbell, Dr. Caldwell Esselstyn, Dr. Michael Greger, and the late Dr. Hans Diehl. Immersing myself in the study of plant-based nutrition added yet another dimension to my life and has had immense benefits on my health ever since.

On my first day of work in Lima, I went to see my friend and my new boss at a Starbucks across from our office. The boss put his three phones on the table in front of me.

"Ravi, your job is to make sure these phones don't ring."

That, friends, was as specific as he got in terms of the job description. Clearly, I knew nothing about the details of his duties but inferred that those annoying phones kept ringing for one reason or another, and he didn't want to deal with answering them himself. The next day, I told him I needed to meet the folks on our team. There were over a hundred people on the project, and I walked around to shake hands with them all.

> I asked every person there one question. "If you had to change one thing on this project, what would it be?"

People shared their feedback while I listened and wrote it all down. It was clear from that meeting that the team was stressed out and had not had a good experience over the past year and a half. They all shared a level of displeasure over how they had been treated by one specific senior member of the team, Stacy, who approached leadership with a top-down, authoritarian style.

That same weekend, an event was scheduled so we could test our systems surrounding implementation and customization of our software product. Development and implementation of telecom software is akin to making a recipe. It's about gathering the right ingredients (codes, designs, user feedback) and following a step-by-step process (developmental phases) to bring your unique dish (the software itself) to life. The goal isn't just to cook something up, but to ensure it tastes incredible and satisfies the needs of the consumer (the user, in this case). This requires a blend of creativity and precision, along with a dash of innovation.

When we implement software at the enterprise level, our best bet is to conduct a dress rehearsal before end users—actual customers—can use it. Just as actors practice their lines and choreography before the real show begins, those of us working in the software industry conduct a final run-through before launching our products.

For our dress rehearsal in Lima, hundreds of team members participated throughout the weekend from 8:00 p.m. Friday until 9:00 a.m. Monday. I gathered our team to plan and strategize our approach. We had a huge whiteboard in our office. I repurposed it as a real-time dashboard for the duration of the dress rehearsal to document any and all issues we might encounter over the weekend, which we would have to correct for the true product launch to go well.

I instructed the team to stay disciplined, calm, and collected, come what may. They all knew in no uncertain terms that I had their back. I made sure everyone was on board with the idea of documenting all issues over the weekend, no exceptions, and divided the board into the following columns:

1. Description of the problem/issue
2. Do we know how to solve the issue onsite? Y/N
3. If yes, what is the solution, and who can execute it?
4. If not, who can solve it from offsite, and what is their contact info?
5. Any miscellaneous comments

That night, a few minutes into the dress rehearsal, we experienced a few issues. Some of our people ran software scripts that caused the database to update certain elements in the wrong order. Stacy, became nervous about this, feeling like our whole project was about to crash and burn. She called me at around midnight to gather all our team members to discuss what had happened. I explained to her that these were minor bugs and missteps the team knew how to resolve and that there was no need to bother team members who weren't assigned to this activity for the weekend.

But she was visibly displeased with my response, used to having her way, and reached out to the head of the Latin American division for the company I was working for, a senior colleague of mine named Joao. I knew him well, and he soon called me to ask what was happening. I ensured him we were simply going through a dress rehearsal, sussing out problems before the product was launched. We wanted to identify what might be wrong with the system and what we could solve before customers got involved.

Over the next few days, I only returned to my hotel to shower and freshen up. Apart from those precious moments, I never left the project. Come Monday morning, some fifty of us gathered in a large, windowless boardroom to discuss our results and lessons learned. Stacy sat at the head of the table while I sat on the other end facing her.

She was upset, adamant that we didn't know what we were doing, pointing her finger at me while she spoke. While she was knowledgeable and technically proficient in our field, her dictatorial behavior rubbed me (and many other people, apparently) the wrong way. I politely told her a couple of times that we would speak to each other professionally or not at all.

She wouldn't hear what I had to say, so I took my laptop, turned it off, and walked out of the room.

My colleagues begged me not to leave the project, and I certainly didn't want to. I'd seen all they'd accomplished over the weekend and had no reason not to respect their work. At the same time, I wasn't going to sit around and accept abuse from anyone. I called Stacy later that day and asked if she could meet for a cup of coffee. She agreed to do so, and we had a heart-to-heart.

"Look," I told her, "I understand you're under pressure, but I'm here to help you. If you don't want my help, there's a flight back to Miami tonight that I can take, but here's my worry for you: I've already spoken to everyone on our team over the past few days. You may not know this, but I received feedback about you, saying you've been giving employees tasks at the end of the day, every Friday, for over a year and a half. This means they can't go anywhere on weekends and have to drop plans they've already made. Our team isn't contracted to work 24/7. If you want my help, I'll do everything in my power to make this project a success, but I will never let a team I'm leading work like this. You have to respect them and honor their time."

Stacy was unhappy to hear my feedback but heard me out, nonetheless. I suggested moving forward that if there were any issues concerning the team, she should reach out to me directly to discuss them, and we would chart out a course of action together. I also told her not to call me in the morning, as she had a couple times, because that was my time to train for the Paris Marathon. She begrudgingly agreed, and ultimately, we sorted out our differences. To her credit, she was a committed leader, and we did incredibly well in the long run, particularly when we went live with the product in April 2010.

I was participating in the marathon at the time, getting updates on my cell phone from the team. The level of trust we had built was a beautiful feeling—almost like being in the state of flow I experienced while exercising.

In the corporate world, there's a lot of lip service about customer success and courageous conversations, but in my experience, very few leaders have mastered the skills required to deal with conflicts between clients and employees. I've seen several team members leave jobs due to a lack of respect and support. They were used, scapegoated by those in charge to fill the gap created by a lack of true leadership. My question is this: Why must we choose between customers and employees? Both are crucial to each other's existence and represent two sides of the same coin. Managing both with respect, integrity, and fairness results in greater satisfaction all around.

Courageous conversations lose their punch when they lack authenticity, sincerity, and action rooted in genuine care for everyone involved.

During my time in Lima, my project extended from a month-long commitment to a year-long stay. This was particularly challenging for my family, as Sasha was only nine and Sahara was just three. I would come home to Atlanta for a couple of days at a time, then leave soon after, driven by the need to support our finances. During those brief visits, the kids would fill every moment with their activities, leaving little time for Lillian and me to connect. This was incredibly hard on her, and my longing to be home with them grew stronger with each trip.

Once I got back to Atlanta for good, I went to my doctor there and showed him my updated cholesterol results, which showed I had brought my cholesterol down to a healthy level without the medication he'd wanted to prescribe.

Ravi's young family, 2011

"Good for you," he said simply.

"Don't you want to know anything else? You're not curious about the cause?"

He laughed, smug and uninterested. At that point, I told him that would be my last time seeing him and never went back, incensed at his manner and lack of professionalism. This was another *inflection point*. It inspired me to devote the rest of my life to understanding nutrition and its impact on our health. I will be forever grateful to that doctor for showing his indifference.

While we humans all carry different conceptions of what's right and wrong, most of us can agree on universal values like respect, consideration, and active listening.

With this perspective, we must focus on winning people's hearts first and foremost. You're not going to win every battle, but that won't matter if you keep that element of faith—the one that knows you're on the right path regardless of the specific outcome. This is how we create relationships with substance. Ones that aren't superficial nor transactional.

To this day, I stay connected with the friends I made in Latin America, and Stacy writes recommendation letters for me. Through our intention to resolve rather than deepen conflict with those in our lives, we create powerful bonds that endure.

"In the midst of chaos, there is also opportunity."

—Sun Tzu, author, *The Art of War*

Most people in this world, particularly those who go through hardship, build a brick wall around their hearts and can come across coldly at first. To break through that wall, you have to take a step back and visualize their point of view. Figure out how to address their concerns without losing your own point of view (or that of your team, if you're leading one). Sometimes you'll succeed at this, sometimes you'll fail, but you have to take a chance and try.

University of Life

LESSON #11: ENERGY AND ATTITUDE

I am energy. So are you. With a can-do mindset, we open ourselves to limitless possibilities. Rarely does life unfold as expected. Building our masterpiece requires the stamina to stay in the game. The energy and attitude we carry helps us navigate all waters. What energy and attitude are you carrying through life?

TWELVE

Riding the Tide

"Life is a matter of choices, and every choice you make makes you."

—John C. Maxwell, American author and speaker

After I got home to Atlanta, my friend, Cris, who had gotten me the job in Lima, invited me to come work in Mexico, but I turned down his offer. I couldn't keep traveling indefinitely anymore, and I wanted to be home with my family. I was able to sign my next contract soon after, this time with a local company. Like the first professional job I was ever offered, I didn't like the gig because there was no energy at the place. Right at the six-month mark, I decided not to renew my contract, sure that it wasn't for me. I needed to be making more money anyway, so I went back to the job market to search for what I wanted.

By chance, my friend Cris reached back out to me from Mexico City again around that time, asking if I wanted to work for the same company I had in Lima. He told me I'd be able to pick whatever role suited me. I signed on to lead implementation in five countries across Latin America, which wouldn't require me to travel full time. I'd be able to work from home, only hopping around when necessary. This felt reasonable, and this time, I gladly accepted his offer. He was the only person in my career who'd ever truly looked out for me on the basis of merit alone.

All the company's telecom work in the five countries I was responsible for was connected, and I led the local teams in getting the job done. At that point, I had the honor of leading a team of around a thousand people. It was fun to handle so many moving parts at once, from contract negotiation to people issues to product-related deliverables. I was managing a huge project in real time, proving to myself once more that I had what it took and had yet to hit the limit of my abilities.

For a good eighteen-month run, things went smoothly. However, a senior member of the company eventually stepped in, and friction arose. He would make big promises that never panned out in relation to things like travel plans, project implementation, the hiring process, and support for employees. This habit of his reminded me of the professor in Milwaukee who had given me false hope for a job in the summer of '89. One day at home in Atlanta, I challenged him on his leadership style and all the fake promises that weren't helping anyone, knowing I would likely lose my job for speaking up. And predictably, I did.

I could have kept my mouth shut and kept making money, but my allergy to his lack of integrity kicked up, and I had to tell the truth.

He had the fancier title, which demanded more of him than mine did of me, but I couldn't continue to accept the way things were.

I was happy I'd been able to execute the way I had for eighteen months, but the time had come for something new. I took a couple days off before getting a call from a recruiter, who offered me an assignment in the mobile workforce software space. Excited at the prospect of learning new skills, I accepted the opportunity to interview, remembering what happened when I let my fear destroy my judgment in London. It went well, and I got the job, excited for fresh knowledge and experiences.

At the time, I was training to run in the New York Marathon for a second time. By then, I had participated in six full marathons in Atlanta, Paris, New York, and Chicago. I logged somewhere between 600 to 1,000 miles while training for each event and paid close attention to my posture, fitness, nutrition, rest, and mindset. Over those years, I managed to reduce my time by an hour and twenty-five minutes, ultimately clocking in at my best time of four hours and thirty-seven minutes in New York. It was an incredible experience, as I was able to cover the final five miles more quickly than any other stretch of the race. My goal was to cross the finish line within four and a half hours, which I missed by seven minutes, but the high of finishing at my fastest is still etched into my soul. Any marathon runner will tell you that any effort beyond the twenty-mile marker hinges on one's training and determination. I left the event knowing I could summon that same energy anytime I faced adversity.

Years of long-distance running had fundamentally rewired my brain, enabling me to maintain focus amid distractions.

A week before my second New York Marathon, I fell and tore my meniscus, an injury that required surgery, and that was where my journey as a marathon runner came to an end. I got the operation and started my new job the following Monday in a cast. As a lifelong athlete, I was devastated. Running had brought me joy like nothing else in the world. The state of flow it created made me feel invincible.

Now, uncertainty loomed over my fitness future. It took time to accept this and pivot toward other activities that might offer similar benefits. Ultimately, I decided on Pilates and did a year of training to become a certified instructor. I also go on daily walks and jump rope. But if I'm honest, whenever I see someone on a run, the desire surges through me. It's yet another opportunity from the universe to practice acceptance of things I can't control and to adapt in order to keep thriving.

During the period from late 2014 to 2016, my youngest daughter, Sahara, began taking horse riding classes. She showed great promise and came alive when she was with the horses. In a short time, she developed a reputation at the stable for being able to ride any horse that others had issues with. Her gentle approach to everything and her ability to connect with the animals was a thing of beauty. They say horses are some of the most sensitive animals and react to the sentiments of the rider. We had a front-row seat to witness this connection.

Sahara's first competition, October 2015

Sahara's second competition, after her win

In October 2015, on a very cold day in Atlanta, at the age of eight, she participated in her very first competition. She was so excited, but she came in dead last in every category. It was hard to see, not just for us parents, but for everyone in the barn. Sitting on her horse, her head steadily went down with tears streaming down her face. It was crushing, but I remember hugging her and telling her that this was the best gift she could have asked for. Now, there was nowhere to go but up.

By March 2016, she competed in her second competition and won every category. But what she did next stunned everyone in the barn and taught us adults a lesson in humility. She got down from her horse, took her winning ribbon, and proceeded to hug all her peers and adults in the barn. Having been at the bottom just a few months before, she didn't want any of her peers to feel discouraged. She acted like it was just another day in the park and made everyone feel appreciated. We were so proud and humbled by her gesture.

Kids have so much wisdom and heart, if only we adults take the time to observe and listen to them.

Despite my sudden forced ejection from the world of marathon running, I continued to attend nutrition conferences to learn more about health between job assignments. In late 2016, I took on a couple of projects at home in Atlanta. Shortly thereafter, the client announced it would be putting on a talent show for employees. I wasn't sure whether contract workers could participate in the event, but I called the guy in charge that morning to ask him.

"Can I participate too?"

"Yes, we'd love it if you did! But what would you do?"

"I'm not sure, but I'll think of something."

I went for a short walk before work and decided I wanted to talk about nutrition. I brought my knives, cutting board, a variety of vegetables and fruits, and other kitchenware with me. I quickly whipped together a dressing with cashews, garlic, and pepper that people tend to love. When I showed up to work, the people in charge asked what they should call me while introducing me to the crowd.

"Call me... The Salad Guy."

I hadn't prepared anything to say, but I walked onstage and winged it. My presentation was so well received that the employees formed a health club to talk about nutrition with one another on a weekly basis. From then on, a

day didn't go by when someone wouldn't stop by to show me what they'd made for lunch or tell me about how they'd made a conscious decision to improve their nutrition.

The experience showed me that the simple act of speaking from my heart about health and nutrition had touched many people. Some would come and tell me about their health problems, grateful that I was helping them get back on track. However, after a few months the club was disbanded by HR. I never understood the reason, but it had something to do with legality.

Although nutrition and health aren't the themes of this book, I'll leave you with the age-old saying, "Food is medicine." I'm certain that had I not learned to value my health, I would not be where I am today. And if I were to die right at this moment, I would want the people I care for to remember me for encouraging them to only consume nutritionally dense food for a vibrant, healthy, and happy life.

> *"As a general rule it almost always happens that when the immediate consequence is favorable, the later consequences are disastrous and vice versa."*
>
> —Frederic Bastiat, French economist and writer

Shortly after that period, my contract ended abruptly in Atlanta, and I had to think hard about what I wanted to do next. Cloud computing was becoming a big thing, and I knew that Salesforce was becoming a huge player in the tech industry. I had written to the cofounder, chairman, and CEO Marc Benioff when he first started the company in 1999 but had never heard back. The time had come to try my luck with the universe again. I took out a sheet of paper and wrote down that I wanted to work there entirely for the benefit of my own mindset, though not specifying in what context.

As luck would have it, my friend Cris called me around that time with an intriguing opportunity. He had just been hired at a startup in San Francisco working on innovative solutions in the telecom industry, all built on the Salesforce platform. He was set to lead a project in Argentina and wanted me to join him. Lilian, who was listening in on the conversation, signaled for me to say "yes."

It was a tough decision because it meant being away from home once again. But we still needed to pay off our bills, and Cris was always reliable. He needed my help, and I couldn't turn him down. Lilian agreed, but I knew this wasn't the first time she had sacrificed her own dreams for my career.

Lilian is remarkable. A self-taught polyglot, she speaks five languages, including English. She is one of the most organized and creative people I know, with an incredible eye for beauty. Thanks to her, our daughters are trilingual. We're not perfect, but we've worked hard to support each other, our children, and our extended family and friends.

I feel fortunate that we've both overcome significant adversity and can relate to each other deeply.

Yet, it remains a challenge for me knowing that my profession has impacted her dreams—a consequence I could never have predicted.

I sent Cris my resume, and he passed it along to his CEO. I began the interview process soon after, which took five months altogether to complete. In December of 2017, I was offered the job, signed the contract, and was on my way to Argentina. Upon arrival, I was presented with a team of young employees working on a project experiencing a number of issues related to conflict management and cultural clashes. Several people had quit before I arrived, and I sensed a lack of trust.

One of the first questions I was asked by many after arriving was, "When are you leaving?" I initially ignored the question but had to address it after a couple weeks. I gathered a group of team members together and asked them point blank why I kept getting this question. They told me several folks who had come before me from the USA had talked a big game but didn't last. The people on my team clearly felt uncared for and abandoned by management.

I took their message to heart, affected by their energy. Bottom line, my team needed a leader who wouldn't walk out on them.

They needed someone who would listen, care, and stick it out with them so they could get through this hard time. At that point, I talked to Cris and the client, saying we needed a different approach to how the project was being handled.

I called a town hall meeting with the entire team. There were over 400 people in the room, and I gave a two-hour talk that had nothing to do with the project. I simply talked about how they could condition themselves toward peak mind and body states every day. "What would you do if you didn't work for this company? How would you lead yourself?" These were life lessons I had learned through experience, read in books, and learned from others I had met throughout life, and I poured my heart and soul into delivering this presentation in the same manner. There was nothing I said that I did not personally practice or believe deep within my soul.

That presentation helped me break the ice, not only with my team, but our clients as well. It was well received, and people insisted I give the same talk to all newcomers to the company. I told the team that I would only leave the project if I was dead or fired by the client or my employer in the US, so they were stuck with me for the foreseeable future.

To establish genuine connections, I took on the mission of daily walks around the floor so I could engage with every team member. It required about three months of unwavering discipline, but eventually, people began approaching me to discuss both personal and professional challenges they were facing.

Soon, I ended up hiring around sixty-five people who worked alongside me nonstop. By Friday of each week, we were exhausted. Over weekends, some of us would meet in Cris's apartment to work on our strategy as a team, and things slowly started to go better with the project.

Not perfect, but better. We began to trust each other and work as a cohesive unit.

By the end of the nine months I worked in Argentina, I'd given five town hall meetings on different topics, like the agile software development framework and game plans for how to move through different challenges together. We built an amazing team of over 600 people who I can reach out to anytime to this day and visit as friends. I give a lot of credit to the owners of the startup company I was working for there, which Salesforce had acquired, for trusting me to run the project how I wanted to without interruption.

During that time, I was leading employees who'd come from politically torn countries like Venezuela. Some couldn't afford to eat every day because they were sending their earnings to their families back home. I had to know what was happening in their lives in order to push them to perform in ways that honored their humanity. So often in the corporate world, driven by greed, ego, and competition, our humanity is defiled rather than nourished.

Nine months after I arrived in Argentina, I said goodbye to my team there, leaving them with tears in their eyes, feeling validated by the small impact I had made there and thankful for their hospitality and reciprocity. Since then, I've continued at Salesforce and had various opportunities to lead different projects.

To be a great leader in those roles, I've never had to be perfect.

I needed to be vulnerable. I needed to listen. I had to have empathy, compassion, and patience with everyone. I needed to truly care. I had to be willing to take a fall for the team, including losing my job if it came to that. I had to be brutally honest with everyone, especially myself. I couldn't pretend to be someone with all the answers and solutions to the challenges of the day. I believe this all helped me build trust with people. Integrity is one of the rarest traits in existence, but we all know it when we see it.

I had manifested my dream of working for Salesforce. That scribble of intention became my reality in 2020 and went on to open doors I'd wanted to walk through for years. Toward the end of the Argentina project, I was optimistic that more leadership roles of that scale would come my way. I had loved the level of responsibility entrusted to me. The large yet closely knit team. All the intricacies that had to be considered and tweaked for the project to run smoothly.

Unfortunately, my upward trajectory plateaued when I realized that taking on top leadership roles with higher pay would likely require me to compromise on some of my principles. I had put blood, sweat, and tears into the work, as always, and was promised a promotion, but things don't work that way at the top.

After so many years of working the grind, I can tell you these types of realizations aren't a signal to give up on your purpose.

Don't drop your standards to conform to the world's expectations of what type of box you should be or which labels to fill it with.

The only "brand" you need to build is your own. Know who you are. Value yourself. If you do this, you'll have gotten further in life than the majority of people ever will. At that point, the corporate world can deny you promotions but not your dignity. Reality will always look different from what we envision. You might not end up getting exactly what you want, even after a lifetime of hard work, but you will know you tried, and you'll learn priceless wisdom along the way.

Moving up in the ranks of most organizations comes with intense levels of interorganizational politics and drama. This toxicity can jeopardize our mental, physical, and spiritual well-being and strain our personal and professional relationships. Navigating such environments gets even more challenging when we're faced with the temptation of greater wealth and prestigious titles.

I eventually arrived at the clear, unwavering decision to give my health precedence over any title or monetary gain, as I can only deliver my best at peak health. There are no right or wrong answers here. You must do whatever works best for you and your loved ones.

University of Life

LESSON #12: KINDNESS AND CARE

No one cares how much you know until they know how much you care. Kindness surpasses skill and intellect in importance. Without these considerations, we are lost, for they are the only true prizes that await us at the end. How do you show kindness and care in your life?

Conclusion

"I looked in temples, churches, and mosques. But I found the Divine within my heart."

—Rumi, poet, theologian, and scholar

In this expansive tapestry of life, I've had the privilege of seeing the world, stepping into the roles of both husband and father, leaving a global impact on those I've encountered, conquering several marathons, and achieving milestones that, in the grand scheme, pale in comparison to the extraordinary people who have shared this journey with me—this *safar*—and their help in shaping who I am and who I am becoming.

Although you've reached the end of this book, no story ever really ends. Life will always come back with more opportunities and curveballs, and I couldn't leave you here without sharing a final plot twist. Just as I was finishing this manuscript, the first week of February 2024 hit me with another blow—I received notice of the elimination of my cherished leadership role at Salesforce as part of a massive corporate layoff. Life's unpredictability was laid bare yet again. But I am here, standing tall, reconnecting with my roots as always, determined to forge ahead.

I didn't write this book to dictate how anyone should be living. My aim has simply been to share my story as it is in hopes of inspiring others as they navigate life's twists and turns. As I've said at many points, leadership is a journey that begins internally, rooted in our willingness to lead from the heart. It's about making continuous decisions and taking responsibility for the outcomes we encounter. It's about acknowledging that we don't succeed alone. We rely on our whole village to help us learn, grow, and thrive. It's about resilience, kindness, courage, persistence, and tenacity. It's understanding that change begins with us.

Life is transient, as are we. We have a small window of time to make the most of our experience on this planet and serve as beacons of inspiration for others. History is littered with people who overcame limiting beliefs about themselves and others, succeeding in ways that will continue to inspire generations to come. Though there are too many to list here, a handful have been especially influential for me throughout my life.

There was Dawn Loggins of North Carolina, a young woman who went from being homeless and working as a janitor at her own high school to graduating from Harvard University on an all-expenses paid scholarship in 2012.

There was Anand Kumar, an Indian mathematics educator who started a school named Super 30 to coach impoverished kids to compete and make it to the famed Indian Institute of Technology.

There was Fuja Singh, who ran his last full marathon at the age of 100 in eight hours and twenty-five minutes in 2011.

Dr. Abdul Kalam, a man born in poverty in southern India, went on to become one of the most admired space scientists in the world, and eventually the eleventh president of my home country.

Sister Madonna Buder, the "Iron Nun," completed an Ironman

Triathlon at the age of eighty-two in 2012, making her the oldest woman to ever finish a triathlon.

There was also Diana Nyad, the first person to swim from Cuba to Florida at the age of sixty-four in 2013.

These incredible folks have demonstrated the power we all possess to overcome the mental stories standing in the way of our own greatness. Every choice we make in life weaves a complex pattern of costs and benefits.

Regrettably, I only fully grasped, articulated, and acknowledged this reality later in my journey. Decisions, once made, can bear heavy consequences, and I reflect with a sense of realization on the impact of my choices. The geographic distance between my family in India and Brazil and my daughters in the USA, a consequence of my decisions, has meant missed moments of togetherness in both joy and sorrow. The warmth of daily life in Brazil, so integral to my wife's heart, was altered when we left her home country. Looking back, it feels like a weighty toll, a sacrifice that was perhaps too great.

Yet amid these reflections, I find solace in the hope that the experiences I've shared with my daughters and wife have crafted a unique and enriching narrative. It's a delicate balance of acknowledging the costs while cherishing the invaluable lessons learned along the way.

In every pursuit, both personal and professional, my compass has been my heart. Every step on this journey has been guided by a commitment to doing the right thing with kindness, a genuine desire to be of help others, and an ability to be comfortable in the midst of uncertainty. I'm happy to have come this far without absorbing the stereotypes and labels of others as part of myself.

To every character, every plot twist, and every poignant moment etched in these pages, I extend my deepest gratitude. I harbor no grudges or bitterness. Those who pass through our lives are always right on time.

As I close this memoir in celebration of all that has happened in my life, I feel I'm being offered the opportunity to leap forward into the unwritten pages of tomorrow, ready for the stories that have yet to unfold. May my story inspire you to maintain an element of faith in yourself as you travel a journey fueled by resilience, passion, and an unwavering commitment to making a meaningful impact. May your own narrative be filled with triumphs, growth, and the enduring pursuit of greatness. Paint your life into a brilliant masterpiece, present for every moment, as if no one was watching at all.

You are where you should be, wherever that currently is, and hold all the keys to your kingdom. May you find the doors meant for you, open them wide, and walk through knowing the inner force guiding you will always find its way. And whatever you do, respect yourself, encourage yourself, empower yourself, never give up on yourself, and believe in your inherent grit.

Only one of you exists in this vast universe. Show them what you've got and make it count.

Acknowledgments

I want to begin by acknowledging my lovely parents, my siblings, my wife and daughters, all my teachers and professors, coaches, extended family members, friends, coworkers globally, and "the village" for the rich life experiences I have been fortunate to have lived through. There are literally thousands of you, and hence, it is hard to list everyone here, but you all know who you are and how I value each and every one of you. Each of you has helped shape who I am and who I am becoming in ways you will not imagine. Yet, there are some standouts I must acknowledge in my life's journey so far:

Dad and Mom, the English language does not have words to truly describe what I feel for both of you. What you have done for me and my siblings. How you guided us with love, care, courage, dedication, and integrity. No challenge was too big for both of you. You set a very high bar and taught us with examples. I can truly say, "I am because you are."

My siblings: Ruby, Rashmi, Shabnam, and Archana. All of you are my pillar. You all had such a profound influence on my life. In my absence in India since 1988, you all have shouldered the responsibilities of taking care of our parents and your own families in ways that are nothing short of exemplary. Again, words cannot describe my love and respect for all of you.

Rajesh Kumar Singh, my cousin, whose love and care has no limits. In my absence from India since 1988, you've been a strong pillar of support for our extended family and have shouldered so many of the responsibilities of taking care of our aging parents and relatives. I honor and respect you forever and will forever remember all the wrestling matches we had as kids.

Peggy Holsclaw, this book would not have been possible without your dedication, attention to detail, and most importantly, your skill in understanding me as a person, author, and storyteller. You did a masterful job of turning my words as an amateur writer into the work of art. Huge thanks to you for your patience and guidance throughout this journey.

Thanks to the late Dr. Harold Beals at the University of Wisconsin, Platteville for taking me seriously when I began communicating with you in 1985. You helped me land a teaching assistantship at the university in 1989 to get my American journey started. In addition, a heartfelt thank you to Prof. John E. Ambrosius, Prof. John E. Cottingham, Prof. Robert Cropp, and Prof. Robert Acton for being amazing teachers, guides, mentors, and human beings. All of you stepped in to help and guide me at some of the most vulnerable moments of my journey in America.

Dr. Meenakshi Maski and Late Dr. Ravikant Maski, you took me in as one of your own from the first day of my life in Platteville, Wisconsin, and helped me assimilate into life in America. You were there for me well past my time in Platteville as well, always ready to provide support. I owe both of you a huge debt of gratitude for being so authentic, loving, and caring. "Thank you" seems too small a phrase for what you did for me and others over the years in that community.

Paras and Lori Reddy, by opening the door to your home on a very chilly night upon my arrival on January 1, 1989, just past midnight, you both made a lasting impression on me. Though I showed up uninvited that first night, you subsequently guided me and my roommate Coomar by your example of hard work and dedication as immigrants. I learned more by observing you than I did during our conversations themselves. Thank you from the bottom of my heart.

Parmeshwar Coomar, thank you for being my very first roommate in America and for always being patient with me. You helped me learn to use computers by teaching me about word processors, floppy disks, and how to save my work. (I'm sure you remember the many times I forgot to save and lost everything!) Thanks for the company and for sharing the early challenges of learning how to drive in America. Thank you for your camaraderie while we were rationing our food to fit our budget. Thanks for lending me your extra bed while I spent time at your place in Milwaukee. I appreciate it all.

To the larger Platteville community, thank you all for accepting me as one of your own during my brief two years there. I am humbled and proud to call it my second home and feel nostalgic just thinking about the place. From the car mechanics who helped me many times without charging me to the police department that helped us find the $150 we lost in downtown Platteville, you all cemented my personal faith in humanity and the goodness that exists inside most people. To all the friends and numerous colleagues I met along the way, thank you for your openness, inclusivity, love, and the care that made starting a new life in America possible.

A huge heartfelt thank you to my mentor and guide at the University of Idaho, Dr. Joseph F. Guenther, whose kindness and insight were touching. He and my entire graduate class of 1992 understood my need and collected the cash that helped me make it to Charlotte in 1992. This may be a small gesture for many, but for me it meant the world. It was yet another example that helped me further strengthen my belief in the goodness of humanity. I also want to thank the entire University of Idaho community for a wonderful two years, which helped me further understand America, its values, and myself as a young man.

Brenda Peters, you helped me get the $2,000 car loan in 1993 that allowed me to continue to dream of a better future. It helped me complete my MBA in Charlotte. You were one of the many strangers who believed in me and helped me along my journey, again cementing my belief that most people want to be good and helpful to others. You have my full gratitude.

Wes Sturges, thank you for taking a keen interest in my final MBA project and for offering me my first professional job. You may not know this, but that meant the world to me at the time, and it cemented my resolve that I was on the right path. Your trust in me, particularly in the city of Charlotte where few people extended any my way, was unbelievable. I still get chills thinking about it. I shall remain grateful for your gesture for the rest of my life.

Robert Cuillare, thank you for believing in me and giving me a job that helped me to learn so much about myself and to continue to dream about a better tomorrow. Your signature line, "I look good, I feel good, and I am good," still resonates with me as I get myself started every day.

Peter and Sampath Chakravarti, thank you for speaking with me in the laundry room and opening the door to the first and second professional jobs that transformed my life. I can't thank you enough, and I feel deeply for both of you.

Cristian Radu, of all the people I've worked with during my career to date, you are by far the only one who took the time to listen, mentor, support, and promote me on merit, time and again. Those opportunities led to self-discovery and personal development in ways that are hard to describe.

Sandhya Krishnan and Nanda Reddy, we met in 1998 at work and our journey continues through the ups and downs of life. I want to thank you both for your generosity and care for me and my family. It's rare these days to meet people who care as much as you both do, and for that, I want to honor and respect you. I am simply grateful for your friendship and trust.

Osler Kamat, my friend and confidant. Thank you for your trust in me and for not hesitating to be a cosigner for the MBA college loan. That transformed my life and again helped me see the value of building trusted and honest friendships and relationships. I honor you, Kamat!

Malik Rafi and Vinay Yallambalse, I will be forever grateful to both of you for being such amazing and trusting friends. Your help in 2007 and 2008 when we were totally broke helped us get back on our feet, and that story continues to this date. You both exemplify what it means to be a genuine, caring, and loving human being.

To the entire AgMaCo class of 1988 at the University of Agricultural Sciences, Bangalore and its faculty, thank you for the wonderful four years on campus. Thank you for your friendship, guidance, love, care, and above all, the teachings that I carry to this date. Each and every one of you played a huge part in who I've become and am becoming. I love and respect all of you unconditionally.

Last but not the least, I owe a huge debt of gratitude to all my beta readers, who took the time out of their busy schedules to share their constructive feedback and suggestions. William Carduner, Vinay Yellambalse, Tim Surr, Taylor Keller, Scot Safon, Ninan Chacko, Lindsay Hua, Kurt Leopoldino, Dr. Nick Morgan, Cris Radu, Ben Pearce, Dr. LeAnne Campbell, Tom Heagney, Diego Garcia, Abson Joseph, Cierra Leopoldina, Parisha Pandey, Joanna Gargiula please know that you all mean a lot to me. Some of you know me very well and some of you met me recently, yet you invested in my endeavor, and for that I shall remain grateful for the rest of my life. Thank you for helping me see things that I had overlooked so as to benefit my readers.

Finally, thanks to my wife, Lilian, and my two daughters, Sasha and Sahara, for putting up with me for so many years. Lilian, I uprooted you from life with your family in Brazil. Many things would not have been possible in my (our) life without you holding down the home front as you have at the expense of your own dream. You have taught me a lot; you have endured a lot, and words fail me in describing my gratitude, love, and respect for you. My daughters, you both have challenged and shaped me as a father with your love, mischief, rolled eyes, and drive in your own unique ways. I love you both very much, and thank you for your influence on how I view life.

About the Author

Ravi Prakash is a beacon of resilience and determination, embodying the belief that true leadership begins with leading oneself.

A naturalized US citizen, he earned multiple graduate degrees and never allowed his circumstances to define him. A lifelong athlete and advocate for healthy living, Ravi pushes boundaries and tests his limits, running marathons and exploring the role of nutrition in overall health.

Having collaborated with thousands of individuals from over eighty countries, Ravi's leadership prowess shines through in his ability to lead globally diverse teams on multi-million to multi-billion dollar projects. He is a relentless force, having worked in leadership roles at some of the world's largest software companies.

As a powerful speaker, he effortlessly connects with audiences, influencing progress with honesty and simplicity.

A devoted husband and father, Ravi is settled in Atlanta, Georgia, where he embraces global travel, writing, reading, and healthy cooking. Inspired by the courage and integrity of his grandparents, who were renowned freedom fighters in India, Ravi strives to emulate their values of resilience, honesty, and courage in both his personal and professional life. His village in India holds historical significance as the starting point of India's independence movement.

Ravi's book is a labor of love, sharing his journey of overcoming life's challenges to inspire others to believe in their own power to create positive change. To connect with Ravi or invite him to speak at events, reach out via email or LinkedIn. Stay tuned for his website, coming soon to further connect with his audience and fans.